Teaching Toward Solutions

A Solution-Focused Guide to Improving Student Behavior, Grades, Parental Support and Staff Morale

Linda Metcalf, PhD

Illustrations by **Ryan Metcalf**

Crown House Publishing Limited
www.crownhouse.co.uk

First published by

Crown House Publishing Ltd
Crown Buildings, Bancyfelin, Carmarthen, Wales, SA33 5ND, UK
www.crownhouse.co.uk

and

Crown House Publishing Company LLC
4 Berkeley Street, 1st Floor, Norwalk, CT 06850, USA
www.CHPUS.com

British Library of Cataloguing-in-Publication Data
A catalogue entry for this book is available
from the British Library.

10 Digit ISBN 1904424074
13 Digit ISBN 978-190442407-9

LCCN 2003102583

Printed and bound in the UK by
Cromwell Press
Trowbridge
Wiltshire

This book is personally dedicated to
my children, Roger Jr., Kelli and Ryan,
and to my husband, Roger.

This book is professionally dedicated to
the teachers I have learned from,
the teachers I have known,
and the future teachers I have taught.

About the Author

Linda Metcalf, PhD, is a licensed marriage and family therapist, a licenced professional counselor, a former junior high school teacher, a school counselor, and currently the coordinator for safe and drug free schools in Mansfield ISD, Mansfield, Texas.

The author of numerous articles on brief therapy with adolescents and children, Dr. Metcalf has written three books: *Counseling Toward Solutions* (The Center for Applied Research in Education, 1995), *Parenting Toward Solutions* (Prentice Hall, 1997), and *Solution-Focused Group Therapy* (The Free Press, 1998).

Dr. Metcalf has worked extensively with school systems throughout the United States, Canada, Australia and the United Kingdom as a consultant in solution-focused brief therapy in addition to working with children and adolescents on school and family issues in private practice.

She lives in Arlington, Texas, with her husband Roger and they are the parents of Roger Jr., Kelli, and Ryan.

Dr. Metcalf is available for workshops and consultations. You may contact her by writing to:

Linda Metcalf, PhD
5126 Bridgwater
Arlington, TX 76017
www.lindametcalf.com
E-mail: dr_linda@ix.netcom.com

Contents

Acknowledgments

This book is a composite of my thoughts from being a student and a teacher and in teaching future teachers. It is an effort on my part to provide new ideas to one of the most important professions. In this book I have taken many risks. It introduces ideas that will challenge some teachers and enhance the thinking of others. The ideas are given with a sincere desire to be helpful.

As with any new idea, there are many people who stimulated my thoughts and gathered their words together to help me present the strategies in this book. They all helped to bring the ideas to life.

Thanks to Larissa Cox, a teacher who captured my son's attention and persuaded him that he could succeed in high school. Thanks to Toy Angell, a student teacher who possesses a skill of relationship building that many of us struggle to achieve for years. Terry Cross, for your story on Jose, thanks for showing how a creative response can change a student's life. To Peggy Ellrod, whose experience shows how far kindness can travel even on the bumpiest of roads, thanks for helping me collect the questionnaires describing the needs of your teachers. To Jim Lieber and Dave Colburn, thanks for expressing what you felt was important to include in this book. To Larry Furmanczyk, thanks again for your wisdom about how we are all searching for The Wizard. Your students are lucky. To Ben Furman, your ideas on reteaming are refreshing and enlightening. Thank you for your friendship and determination to simplify ways to build teams, even in schools. To Ina Crowe, a school counselor extraordinaire, thank you for your inspiration and clever ideas to reach teachers in novel ways. To Doug Cook, an elementary school counselor whose school program is a model for reaching and teaching the youngest of students, thank you for your contribution. To Judy Martin, who saw a need and did something about it, thanks for contributing and teaching us all what a CHUM can do.

To the best editor ever, Connie Kallback, thanks for always believing in what I do and what I write about! Thanks to my office staff, Tami and Celeste who are always supportive and my friend Chip Chilton for his encouragement and brainstorming sessions about students.

Finally and most important, thanks to my husband, Roger, Roger Jr., Kelli, and to Ryan, my favorite illustrator.

About This Resource

Teaching Toward Solutions is a handbook written for beginning, experienced, and preservice teachers at all levels who desire to use a more positive, solution-focused approach with their students. The ideas developed in this resource will serve as a companion to *Counseling Toward Solutions* (The Center for Applied Research in Education, 1995), and together, the two books present a complete and comprehensive school program that focuses on student abilities and competencies instead of their misbehaviors and failure. Additionally, the book *Parenting Toward Solutions* (Prentice Hall, 1997) further supports the efforts of faculty and administration within the program, serving parents with an informative guide that describes the same approach utilized by the school.

The entire program stresses noticing "exceptions", or the times when problems *do not occur* and explains how those times give educators clues to use as they develop a different context that is more successful for their students. Developing such a new focus means looking at students and parents differently and taking an introspective look at ourselves as educators, examining our thoughts and beliefs about education and people. Our perspective and perception of who we are and the task given to us each day is essential to instigating change within the classroom. That perception, coupled with renewed parental information, creates a *solution-focused* system in which students and parents begin to have more opportunities to become responsible for their own actions *and their own solutions!*

This book will give teachers and administrators an opportunity to re-examine their roles and develop new ones that will affect their students and faculty members positively, creating an atmosphere of change and competency that will be contagious. Each section will contain information on the following:

- Examples for using solution-focused theory with specific behavioral problems, emotional stressors, parent-teacher conferences, learning difficulties, psychiatric diagnoses, and special education issues.
- Case studies with simple summaries of "What happened here?" will be illustrated throughout each section to clarify the solution-focused ideas so that teachers can examine and learn practical applications that are clear and simple to use.
- A section practice exercise will be presented at the end of each section for the teacher to "solution solve". These activities will assist the education professor, student teacher, or experienced teacher in gaining a new focus in the classroom.

The various techniques and strategies presented in this book have been developed by the author for teaching student teachers and experienced teachers this new approach over the past ten years. Teachers are shown how approaching classroom situations differently can change the behaviors of students and the atmosphere of the classroom.

The Individual Sections

Beginning with a dramatic case study by a new teacher who was determined to give a student one last chance, Chapter One describes new, guiding ideas and assumptions to use in the classroom that create a motivational atmosphere. Other never-before-described strategies help teachers to stop student misbehavior before it begins, creating respect and a responsible climate between student and teacher. This new alliance between teacher and student will keep future misbehaviors minimal. The ideas invite the teacher to think differently about his or her students, developing new behaviors as the perceptions evolve. The ideas/assumptions actually serve as life skills and give teachers the opportunity to not only learn the ideas for their own personal and professional lives, but also to teach them to their students and parents. The "Exceptional School Program" adapts quite easily to the classroom since it focuses on the same goals that schools were always intended to promote: competency, respect, and responsibility within each student.

Chapter Two focuses on assisting teachers to learn to identify their own abilities in solving past problems in the classroom and use such resources in their school. Language defines us and our students. Learning how we handle conflict, crises, offensiveness, anger, and disappointment can help us and also help our students in the classroom to see us as real, respectful people. Our assumptions affect how we handle student conflict—and changing these assumptions can change the outcome of many conversations! Chapter Two lists a specific process for teachers to take when intervening with students on their behalf. The importance of documenting a teacher's perceptions towards his or her students will astonish even the most experienced teacher and will serve as a simple, quick, and effective way to get attention from the most difficult student in the classroom. This section suggests new ways to think about goal setting with students and assists them in writing a new "school story". By understanding that the "*problem* is the problem"—not the student—today's teacher will be able to quickly stop a conflict by helping his or her student to ignore "the problem" and, together, escape from its influence.

Chapter Three examines the thinking and actions of the challenging student. Actual examples from teachers who have used solution-focused techniques to lessen resistance and gain cooperation are described and explained thoroughly. Summaries of each case further the educator's understanding toward a solution focus rather than a problem focus. This section also explores more specifically how to converse with students of all ages and abilities differently so that conflict is replaced by collaboration and respect. The section includes "Guiding Questions" in many formats, ready to copy and use for many situations including how to develop lesson plans that work for particular classrooms, and how to conduct more positive, effective team meetings, teacher/counselor meetings, and parent/student conferences that are solution focused.

Chapter Four presents the "Exceptional School Program" to encourage the educator to become part of the team with administration and the school counselor/psychologist/diagnostician. In this section, the nuts and bolts of running a solution-focused classroom and creating a positive atmosphere are presented through the multiple reproducible forms offered, ready to duplicate and apply immediately to parent conferences, individual education plans, diagnostic meetings, and much more.

Sometimes noticing abilities and competencies in academically challenged students is difficult and teaching them takes perseverance for the regular classroom teacher. Steps for teachers to take to identify these abilities are listed in Chapter Five and give teachers examples of successful students who, when guided by educators using this approach, became successful in their own right. Also included are targeted forms for teachers to fill out to help bring out the best in even the most challenged students, and help them to develop a new attitude. The section also includes questions to ask colleagues that solicit strengths of students, rather than their weaknesses, so that teachers have additional information to help them identify successful strategies that colleagues have discovered work with their shared students. Parents are included in this section as important sources of information for the regular classroom teacher. This method of researching abilities instead of deficits allows the creation of a new system in which the student can immerse himself or herself more positively. The suggestions given in Chapter Five are geared to elementary or secondary situations.

Chapter Six shares valuable information on student issues from childhood depression, anger disorders, ADD, conduct disorders, and a gathering of other labels and diagnoses that teachers must deal with daily. Today's student presents enormous challenges, and this section discloses how successful teachers have worked with parents, counselors, and psychologists to create a unified system that compels students to become more successful. Whether the children in your classroom are dealing with learning differences, sexual abuse, divorce, death and loss, this section is the reference that will take you through difficult times and help you to step into the troubled student's world. There will be suggestions for teachers at the end of each diagnosis so that working with the troubled student becomes less worrisome and more confident, sending a message of safety to the student.

Chapter Seven uses as its premise a quotation that is at the heart of this book: "Some people think you should fight fire with fire … funny, I always use water" (Howard Gossage). Looking at situations differently helps student attitudes to dissolve so that they can become more compliant people. Even Albert Einstein talked about how "you cannot solve a problem with the same kind of thinking that created it". Instead of thinking how a student is "testing" a teacher, teachers are invited to understand what the testing does for the student. Does it mean he/she needs to be in charge of an event, time, or help pass out papers while discussing a joke? Does it mean a teacher needs to change or improve his or her relationship with the student at lunch or after school? Whatever the case, disciplining today's students is vastly different from what it was during the past thirty years. Too many influences have changed and evolved that have helped to deteriorate the teacher-student relationship. This section provides the teacher with several new strategies and ideas to alter the temperament of even the most volatile student.

Chapter Eight gives the classroom teacher an opportunity to teach one more subject— social competency. Whether the students are elementary or secondary, there are exercises and suggested topics that will encompass even the most volatile of schools. Teaching our students how to survive in the world without fighting to the end is the goal of "Conflict Resolution, Solution-Focused Style". This material assists the classroom teacher in assisting his or her students to solve their own problems. This new approach dissolves anger and resistance and opens the door for students to a way of thinking that is nonblaming and more collaborative.

Chapter Nine offers administrators the necessary tools to create a new vision for their school. Included are guidelines for leading a faculty to a new way of thinking theoretically. Additionally, there are handouts for the administrator to copy and hand out to minimize paperwork and maximize thinking. Administrators who have tried program development in the past will be surprised at this section's organized approach to leading people. Based on research by the author, the section contains planning and strategizing used by America's top companies to motivate and inspire their employees—a way to teach and reach today's faculties.

The solution-focused educator does not let the world's problems overtake her enthusiasm for teaching her students a better way to build their world; rather, she focuses on the times when the world has worked better and sees those times as exceptional. The solution-focused teacher does what works. Best wishes to you!

Linda Metcalf

Chapter One
The Solution-Focused Classroom

"There are two kinds of people in the world: those who come into a room and say 'Here I am!' and those who come in and say 'Ah, there you are!' "

—Pearls of Wisdom, Anonymous

She was the kind of teacher who stayed late after school. Her students never described her as an easy teacher, yet she was often seen talking with at least two students whenever she walked down the hall. They loved being around her. They described her as nice, friendly, fair, and kind. She was always asked to sponsor a club or attend dances as a chaperone. She loved her students and her job and her actions showed it.

He was the kind of student who some would say had little hope for a productive future. He had a short attention span, rarely participated in class discussions, and too often did not turn in his homework. At age 17, as a high school senior, Tom had built a reputation that had not earned him many breaks. An average student, he had barely passed most of his classes because of his lack of preparation. He could pass tests but turning in homework was another matter. Too much trouble. He had more important things to do, like working at a part-time job at night to earn money to buy things his family couldn't provide. However, in the spring, his motivation at school increased on the track field after school. He was the fastest member of the track team, with an attitude for winning that was unstoppable.

When Tom's coach came into Ms. Jordan's classroom that afternoon, a week before the state track finals, she was deliberating over the five points Tom needed to pass his French class. The coach, following state rules that required passing grades in order to participate in extracurricular activities, told her to fail him. Ms. Jordan struggled with that decision. She knew that Tom's family was poor, that his parents were divorced, and that he struggled to keep a part-time job at night. He was often tired in the morning, although he had always been polite to her in class. She had seen him perform on days when he felt better and she had prompted him continuously during class, sometimes standing by his desk for most of the class period. When she would remind him to turn in the papers he had completed in class, he did. She knew he had the ability and had seen the pride in his eyes when he scored well on a test.

Ms. Jordan also knew that Tom had an opportunity for a track scholarship, and that such an opportunity might give him a future. He had placed in the last two state track meets and the track coach had told her that if he won as a senior, he would have a sure chance at a full scholarship. She knew that he would be the first person in his family to attend college. Somehow, "teaching him a lesson" for a poor grade did not fit. She saw him as someone in need of being given a chance. Her thinking turned to the question of "what is my goal for this student?" She saw him in need of someone to believe in him more than he needed someone to give him "a consequence". She told the coach she was going to pass him in French.

Tom won the state track meet. He also passed French. For a student who was quiet, his keyboarding teacher was rather surprised a few days later when, looking over Tom's shoulder during class, he noticed that Tom was writing the letter appearing on the next page to Ms. Jordan.

Ms. Jordan, a teacher in Arlington, Texas was a first-year teacher at that time, earning additional certification when she taught Tom. Like all of us, she had hopes and dreams for all of her students, although she was often disillusioned by the expectations to follow certain educational/disciplinary plans that did not always "fit" with her instincts of how to be the most helpful to students. Too often those plans did not work with the more troubled student. Instead, she preferred to think of the times when students like Tom learned best, focusing on those times as solutions and not searching for reasons *why* they did not perform. When she relayed Tom's story as her case study in front of 100 other education students several years ago in one of my university classes, she asked the class:

"Did I do the right thing?"

The class responded with silence. I saw puzzled looks on 50 percent of the class while I applauded her. Statements and questions of teacher consistency, authority, fairness to other students, rules, regulations, and policy were discussed at length by my students after Ms. Jordan presented her successful case. The class exploded with questions:

"How can we get away with doing such creative interventions?"

"Could promoting and encouraging students really be this simple?"

"I think it is incredible what she did. Can you imagine what might happen if other teachers took such an individual approach? Kids might feel understood and cared about!"

"More power to you. She took a risk with a student . . . that's what I thought we were supposed to do."

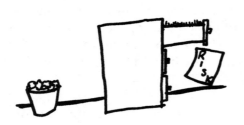

Could noticing that a student was competent, even slightly, and allowing that observation to carry through in conversations and—then actions—result in new, personal interventions that could make such a difference? It sounded like a description of the perfect educational environment. It sounded too simple. Why, then, did the class struggle with *how* to implement the ideas? Ms. Jordan did not break any rules. She merely created an opportunity for Tom to see himself differently and then behave differently as a result. When she returned a week later with the letter from Tom and read it aloud, she won over more support and gave me an opportunity to start a class discussion on new ways of managing classrooms. Her thinking was clear. To encourage and

Ms. Jordan

I know that helping me the way you did has set you back a few steps, but me and my future THANK YOU. I promise you that your effort to help will not be taken advantage of; but will be used to do bigger and better things in French and all my other classes. Besides thanking you I would like to apologize for the trouble I have been all year. Most of all I apologize for putting you in a stressful situation. I came to you not to receive a grade, but to get

extra work and that's still what I would like to do. I feel really low for putting you through this and it will NEVER happen again. After seeing how it was effecting you I came back to your room to tell you that failing was strictly my fault and for you not to worry, but I couldn't find you and then ten minutes later coaches told me that I could run. You know my life is kind of sad. God gave me the skill to run, jump, catch, and think but unfortunately I only use the thinking process on the field. Over the years it has been engraved in my head that being a great athlete is my way through life, so I really don't know how to study. Much of my problem is I don't like to ask people for help unless I've done something to deserve help. See I've done a lot for Katie that's why I feel comfortable asking her for help. I just believe in being independent and that's not doing anything but hurting me so I'm doing my best to change that. Again, I THANK YOU for your help and you will soon see the results.

Tom K.

promote competency and a belief in a student whose work was below average required a different approach and different manner of thinking to make a difference!

Listening to future teachers discuss and process the *solution-focused ideas* that had encouraged Ms. Jordan to try something *different* with Tom was exciting. I had hinted at the solution-focused ideas from the beginning of the semester, interspersing them with educational foundations for discipline, planning, and class management. Talking differently about varied situations, I had noticed that many of the students were intrigued with a new option for reaching and teaching students who needed something besides consequences. They liked the personal, positive touch to the conversations. So I asked them:

"If you were to use in the classroom some of the relationship skills that your friends and family would consider to be important traits of yours, what would you do?"

The following responses of the students reminded me that within each of them was a sincere motive to bring out the best in their students:

"I would stay positive, so that the conversation would be friendly."

"I would have to stay flexible and look at each student individually."

"I would have to take extra time to think about what I was trying to achieve and plan accordingly, individually."

"I would assume that the student was a good person who just needed extra encouragement. . . . I would watch for his or her strengths and capitalize on it by assigning projects that interested the student and that he or she could achieve."

"I like thinking of what the student does versus what he or she does not do. The atmosphere changes when you think that way."

Thinking with a solution focus and their own relational skills expanded their options because the solutions were within themselves and their students. They were no longer limited to rewards and consequences. Instead, they realized that there were a multitude of solutions in each dilemma they would be faced with in the classroom. They only needed to focus differently.

The different approach of the solution-focused teacher

The *solution-focused* teacher approaches problems differently, as Ms. Jordan did, with a desire to look at her student's competencies instead of his deficits. She does not solve problems for students or parents; she lets the student's competencies guide her to solutions. She sees her task as helping the student to identify his abilities through observations. In fact, his abilities are all that she looks for; she does not mention the deficits. This approach lends itself to a more collaborative relationship that often results in a student feeling as if the teacher is on his side. What makes it different from a purely *behavior modification* approach is that the teacher does not compliment just when the student does well, as if only to praise or reinforce him, she compliments the student from a stance of amazement, curiosity, and discovery. Observe the differences in the following statements. The first are made with a *behavior modification* approach and the second with a *solution-focused* approach.

A behavior modification approach

Elementary: Class, you have all behaved very nicely this afternoon. I am going to let you have ten extra minutes in the science center because you have been so quiet.

4

High School: Sue, I know you are a good student and I enjoy having you in my class. However, your homework grades are low in Biology but your tests are passing. You must bring up your homework grade to pass this semester.

Athletics: Guys, good practice at football today. You did much better than yesterday.

Special Education Class: Charlie, you stayed in your seat nicely this morning—there have been no conflicts with Jonathan this morning like yesterday. Good for you! You are on your way to getting a reward this afternoon when school is over.

A solution-focused approach

Elementary: Class, you are amazing. (Circulates in the classroom.) Suzie, I am so impressed with the way you shared with Tommy. Lee, I have never seen any cell drawing as creative as yours. Jimmy, you sat so still in your seat throughout this entire lab. How are you all doing your work so efficiently today? (Waits for answers.) You all have earned ten extra minutes at the science center this afternoon.

High School: Sue, your test grades are excellent. I notice in my grade book that you turned in more homework assignments the first six weeks of this semester. What were you doing then that helped you to turn in the assignments? What were we doing in class that helped you to complete them?

Athletics: Guys, I can't believe your performance today! How have you turned this team around this afternoon?

Special Education Class: Charlie, I am amazed at you today! I've noticed how you sat in your chair and did not allow Jonathan to distract you! Wow! How have you done this?

The second group of questions made the students experts of their behaviors. They were viewed by the teacher as totally responsible for their success. Students and parents are aware of a teacher's training and a look of puzzlement or amazement by a teacher towards her students or parents is a huge compliment! When students think they have done something that the teacher cannot explain or understand, it becomes very motivating. It seems to be an age-old tradition that students challenge their teachers—why not cooperate with that tradition?

How solution-focused statements motivate

In order to further understand how thinking with a solution focus is different from simply being *positive*, it is helpful to compare a problem-focused approach with a solution-focused approach in reference to motivation. The following statements are *problem-focused* strategies often used by teachers to get students motivated to do their work, to pay attention, make better grades, or live up to their potential. As you read them, listen for any solutions or strategies:

Problem-focused motivational strategies that do not work

"Sue, You have the ability, you just need to apply yourself."

"Josh, I am sorry you have chosen to not turn in your assignments in my class. You knew when the assignments were due and it was up to you to do them."

"When you are ready to work, Jamal, let me know. I will be here to help you, but you have to decide to do the work."

"I hope you came prepared to work today, Diane, you are failing this class."

"Kay, I cannot tolerate your misbehavior in class any longer. The next time I catch you talking when I am giving out the assignment, you are going to the office."

What were the solutions or strategies offered in these scenarios? None. The students were simply told what they were doing wrong. All of these statements have been relayed to me by students who said that the statements made them *feel worse*. What is interesting, too, is that each student knew what he or she was doing wrong. The story I continued to hear from the student and the student's parents were that they called the teacher and asked for ideas of what they could do at home. In some cases, the parents did not even call because they were not interested enough in their child's performance and felt that their son or daughter needed to change first. The student did little to raise her grades and when her attitude became even more despondent, it became contagious to the other students. The teacher then probably felt either like a failure and referred the student to the counselor or special education program, or resolved to wait until the student *decided* to try. Maybe the teacher even decided that until she saw the student trying, *she* would not try to help the student. This process failed everyone.

Before the solution-focused teacher talks to a student in trouble academically, she thinks about what her goal is for the student's academic career. The teacher tries to change the context from one of failure (problem focus) to hopefulness (solution focus). The solution-focused teacher looks for competency until she finds it, even if it is minimal, and talks to the student differently. Notice how the former statements change when a new focus is used.

Solution-focused motivational strategies that do work!

"I looked at my grade book this morning, Sue, and I realized that you have passed four out of the last six tests. I also found that you routinely turn in library assignments. When you put your mind to it, you certainly are successful. I wonder how you might approach the last test of this semester on Friday, so that your ability shows on your report card?"

"Josh, I have noticed how responsible you are in taking care of your little brother when you walk to school. I have also watched how you always remember to take care of the aquarium in our science class. You certainly are a responsible fifth grader! You have also turned in your homework for the last two days. I'm quite impressed. What would you suggest to do so that you remember to bring in your homework assignment again tomorrow?"

"Jamal, I'm interested in helping you catch up on your Geometry grade. Your first two six weeks' grades were B's which tells me that you have ability to pass this class with a good grade. Looks like you have gotten slightly off-track at the moment. What did we do in class before that helped you to stay on track? What did you do then that helped you?"

"Diane, your grade of 67 is so close to passing . . . you are only three points away. I remember last semester how you brought up your grade when you really paid attention by sitting up close in the classroom. I wonder if that would help now to help you get those three points."

The teacher asks Kay to step out of the classroom for a moment—partially through the class period before she gives the assignment for the class—and says: "Kay, I appreciated how you came into class this morning and listened to the first few instructions. It helps me to teach you when the class listens. You are a very important student in my class. I wanted you to know that I appreciated your efforts."

Notice how there is now more of a collaborative conversation happening between the teacher and student. It is more than just a positive or reinforcing response. In the solution-focused responses, the student is asked to be the expert; in the problem-focused responses, the teacher describes the problem and then decides the strategy. The trouble with some problem-focused strategies is that they are someone else's and may not be those that the student can perform or want to perform. In the solution-focused responses, the teacher simply observed times when the student exhibited competency of some sort and relayed those times to the student in a caring and curious manner. The delivery of that information is the key. Then the strategies become those of the student's and are more likely to be performed.

Ms. Jordan's approach to helping Tom pass French was a different experience for him. She focused more on his past abilities instead of the current dilemma and relayed the way that she had seen him pass previously. He wasn't used to being given a chance to earn five more points. He was used to being told that he performed poorly and should just bring up his grades. He was caught by surprise by Ms. Jordan's *belief* in him and his resistance faded, allowing motivation to surface instead. Ms. Jordan was willing to take a new approach with Tom that could send a message of confidence to him. This new belief in himself, promoted by his teacher, motivated him like no other intervention had done previously. When Tom found that his teacher believed in him enough to take such a chance with him, he began to take on more responsibility himself, probably feeling quite important in the process. Creating such an atmosphere for Tom required Ms. Jordan to think and plan the solution-focused strategy outlined here.

Developing solution-focused strategies

1. **"What is my goal in working with this student?"**
   Answer: To assist him in believing in his abilities so that he can perform well academically and pass the class.

2. **"When in the past has this student responded to this class effectively?"**
   Answer: When he was prompted, conversed with before an assignment, and encouraged to turn in work on time, he responded positively by getting back on task and completing his work. He passed all of his tests when we reviewed in class.

3. **"When else has the student shown abilities to make passing grades? How often, which assignments did he pass, and what do his successes tell about his abilities?"**
   Answer: The student passed the first semester. He passes his tests, yet often forgets his homework. He has the ability, he just seems to need additional attention. That attention takes a total of two to five minutes per class period.

4. **"How can I share my discovery of his successes with him effectively, so that he hears the successes and is motivated by them? How can I assist him in re-discovering his successes personally?"**
   Answer: I can show my belief in him by examining with him his past success as shown in the grade book and then give him the opportunity to continue his abilities through teaching/assigning him projects or assignments that he has shown an ability to complete.

5. **"How can this process begin on a small scale so that Tom can be more successful?"**
   Answer: I can ask Tom what is helpful to him after I share my observations. I will give him the chance to earn five points, through extra work, and will share with him that I believe he can do it because he has before.

The strategy used by Ms. Jordan did not require a time-consuming glance backward at cumulative folders to try and figure out why Tom was failing, nor did it require an uncomfortable confrontation with Tom and his parents. Most important, it did not demand that Ms. Jordan come up with new strategies for learning. Tom could be successful. He had proven it previously in the school year. It was more probable that Tom would carry out a strategy that he realized he had done before rather than one Ms. Jordan suggested. All she had to do was capitalize on those instances when Tom passed, relay those discoveries to Tom, and be there to assist and encourage him with amazement. (See the reproducible worksheet for teachers to use while brainstorming strategies using a solution-focused approach.)

Developing Solution-Focused Strategies

A Worksheet for Teachers

1. What is my goal in working with this student?

    _____

    _____

    _____

    _____

2. When in this class has the student responded effectively?

    _____

    _____

    _____

    _____

3. When else has this student show ability to make passing grades? How often, which assignments did he or she pass, and what do the student's successes tell about his or her abilities?

    _____

    _____

    _____

    _____

4. How can I share my discoveries of the student's successes effectively, so that he or she hears the successes and is motivated by them? How can I assist the student in rediscovering his or her successes personally?

    _____

    _____

    _____

    _____

5. How can this process begin on a small scale so that the student will be successful?

    _____

    _____

    _____

    _____

Making the student the expert **does** *work!*

Research has suggested that when clients describe their reason for seeking help and are given an opportunity to work on *exactly* what *they* came for—not what the "expert" thinks they should work on—the clients leave more satisfied (Metcalf & Thomas, 1994). If a teacher cannot enlist a student to succeed, the intervention becomes a tug of war at that point. Ways to accomplish helping the student to become an expert on his or her school life are by asking questions such as the following.

The miracle conversation

"How would you like things to be in school?"

"Let's suppose that a miracle happened when you went to sleep tonight and you awoke tomorrow to find that your school life was much better. What would be different at school? How would that be helpful to you?" (De Shazer, 1988)

"Who would notice when school worked for you? What would their seeing that do for you?"

Sometimes, students and parents insist on digging deeper into the problem in an attempt to identify "what's causing the problem". This is quite common. The solution-focused teacher understands the need of the parent or student and cooperates with their view by saying:

"What would it do for you to know why Jonathan can't read well?"

"Suppose there were no other programs for Jonathan. Based on his past or slight successes in his other classes, what would you suggest that he begin to do on a small scale?"

"As his parent, you know him best. Think about what works in other areas of his life to motivate and encourage Jonathan. What would you suggest I do , as his teacher?"

"What would you suggest doing at home to help him, based on any other times when you are able to reach him?"

These questions place responsibility on those who have the closest contact with the student. Instead of "passing the buck" to the teacher, the parents and students have little recourse but to develop a plan. At this point, the teacher can suggest ways that the student seems to learn best, even if slightly, by glancing at her grade book and observing classroom behaviors that are more acceptable. Sharing this information lessens resistance with parents and students alike, again changing the relationship and promoting the atmosphere and perception that the teacher is there to promote success. The classroom begins to run smoother and corrections are made more easily when the atmosphere promotes one of competency—not confrontation—because it also sends a message of respect to students. Then, confrontation from students simply happens less over time. Instead of pointing out what is *not* working, the solution-focused teacher looks for what is working, making her students acutely aware that the classroom is a place to feel *important*. A student who feels important is a student who is motivated and respects the teacher.

The following guidelines for using a solution-focused approach in the school setting will promote a better understanding of how to use solution-focused strategies in the classroom. As the guidelines are described, remember that these ideas are more than just strategies or questions. The ideas are a new way of perceiving, thinking, and then acting *differently*, so that you have the opportunity to see resources in yourself and your students that will steer them toward success. The guidelines were adapted from the work of O'Hanlon and Weiner-Davis (1989).

Guidelines for using a solution-focused approach in the school setting

Using a nonpathological approach offers more options

Looking into classrooms today, children and adolescents are often described as depressed, hyperactive, emotionally disturbed, angry, anxious, chemically dependent, physically abused, or victims of family violence. Viewing such students with these problem-focused labels inhibits both the student and themselves because of a perception that grows from the labels suggesting that "he or she can't". For example, a student who is labeled as ADHD (Attention Deficit Hyperactivity Disorder) can also be perceived as a very energetic student.

"Jon, the energy is keeping you from doing your worksheet. I noticed when you sat alone this morning at the table near the center, you completed your sentences. Where would you suggest going now so that you can finish this assignment?"

This change of perception and conversation suggests two things:

1. The energy is something controllable.

2. Jon will finish his worksheet.

Even if Jon is a student who rarely completes his assignments, talking to him differently will give him a different impression of himself, as if the energy is an entity outside of him, instead of his "being" a problematic student because of the energy.

It is not necessary to promote insight in order to be helpful

What are the differences in the following two questions, formulated to motivate a student to complete homework?

"You are failing social studies. I do not understand what is wrong. Do you? You are barely passing your tests and your projects are unacceptable. Is there something going on that I need to know?"

"Have you ever gotten slightly off track in another class? Tell me how you were able to get back on track."

The first question is a confrontation; the second question suggests that a student might already have some answers to the concern. It is more productive to look at past successes and encourage the student to understand how he or she was able to produce before. When a teacher carries out a lesson plan that encourages all students to be on task and respond with enthusiasm, future lesson plans should be modeled after it. Ask yourself, "What was it about the way I taught this unit to my third-period class on Tuesday that seemed to make such a difference?" The answers are in the successes; you can even ask your students—they will tell you!

It is not necessary to know a great deal about the complaint

Your students spend more waking hours conversing with you than they do with their own parents or family. Some students even go for days without seeing their hard-working parents. While your time can scarcely be spent in understanding all of your students' home lives, you can still be helpful to them by conversing in a solution-focused manner.

For example, a kind teacher once related a story to me about a seventh-grade student from a neglectful home who repeatedly clung to the teacher whenever she felt tearful. The teacher attempted to talk to her about the "sadness" and the student kept silent. Eventually, the teacher simply talked of times when her own daughters were young and how they often became sad. She told the student that it was fine if she needed attention at times, even if she did not want to talk about the problem. The teacher then focused on times when the "sadness" seemed less and commented on it to the student. Eventually, the student seemed to need less attention and talked more easily. This cooperation seemed to lessen the resistance, and the teacher was helpful without knowing details!

Students and parents have complaints, not symptoms

I met once with a divorced parent of a ten-year-old boy who was concerned that his son had a dreadful mental disorder. His son would have "crying outbursts" whenever he did not get his way or was asked to do something he did not like. The son never had outbursts at school, or when he was doing something enjoyable. The father tended to be quite liberal in his parenting style and would give the boy many choices from which to choose when he became upset. Usually the father would stop his own activities to tend to the boy's outbursts. The outbursts occurred frequently at bedtime and before visiting the boy's mother, who had remarried a man who tended to have a more rigid parenting style.

Working with the father in a solution-focused way, I began mentioning that it was interesting that his son rarely had outbursts at his mother's house or at school. I wondered out loud what that meant about those environments. I asked his father to also watch for times when the outbursts did not happen. He mentioned that on occasion when he does not have time to totally tend to his son, the outbursts did not last so long. However, he worried that they were "caused" by something. I then asked the father to consider thinking a little differently for the next week, as if the outbursts were simply a refusal to do something unpleasant instead of an outburst due to a mental problem. I then met with both parents once to focus on other "exceptions". The father began to realize that the outbursts occurred mostly at his house. Within one week, the father changed his behaviors from offering choices to seeing his son as simply refusing to do things. The son stopped the outbursts.

Students and teachers are more motivated when they define their own goals

Notice how simple the answers are to the following statements typically made by students. The answers were simply composed by respecting and then echoing back the students' concern, adding a question to elicit their responsibility and competency.

Statement: I wish Mr. Patton would just get off my back.

Response: I'll bet you do! What would he say you could to do to get him to lay off?

Statement: If Ms. Latierre would just call on me more often, I would do better in her class. I don't think she likes me.

Response: I know you want her to like you. What would be a small sign you could watch for during the day tomorrow that would tell you she liked you just a little?

Statement: School is so boring. What will I ever use chemistry for anyway? I just want to pass it so my parents don't get upset.

Response: Sounds like a good reason. What do you think it will take for you to begin passing chemistry?

Statement: My parents just don't understand how difficult AP English is. I don't know how to explain to them that I am overwhelmed.

Response: How have you managed to talk to them before about things that bothered you?

Notice how simple the answers become when the teacher focuses on the obvious ... that the student has succeeded somewhere in the past. Students who stay in school and are routinely promoted have succeeded. Students in special education programs who raise their scores slightly have succeeded. Students who are in trouble three times a week are out of trouble two times a week.

A snowball effect can occur when one person makes a change

A determined high school teacher told the story of two high school students who had decided to quit school. Before they quit, they openly vowed to make their teachers' lives quite miserable. They would come into class and be quite disruptive. The teacher, meeting with her colleagues, suggested that each teacher write a note to each boy once a week and discreetly give it to them when they came to class. It was a last attempt on their part to keep the boys in school. The notes consisted of anything the teachers could muster to write about:

"You came into my class today and it was good to see you. Thanks for sitting down for a few minutes and listening."

"I appreciated your 'hello' this morning. I had a rough morning and it helped."

"You remind me of a bright student I had a few years ago . . . he wasn't quite sure how to show me his abilities at first, but I knew he had lots of potential. Whenever you are ready to show me, I'm here."

The students never dropped out of school. They began to settle down in the classroom, and the teachers took the extra effort to meet with them individually to help them with their work.

Complex problems do not have to necessitate complex solutions

Kenny, age twelve, had been given every medication for his ADHD during the first seven years of his school life. Eventually, Kenny's doctor found two medications that seemed to help, yet his teachers continued to be concerned about his lack of organization and his tendency to not hand in his homework.

When I met with Kenny and his mom, Kenny brought his new binder (one of many that his mother had purchased for him over the years). Roaming around my office, Kenny finally stopped

long enough to show me the binder. Inside were eight dividers, all empty except for the "Band" divider, which had every paper Kenny had received in band since the beginning of the year.

LM: Kenny, this is incredible. Tell me, what is it about Band that helps you to save your papers?

K: I like band.

LM: So when you like something, you pay attention to it?

K: Sure.

Kenny's mom continued to talk about how Kenny didn't seem to worry about his homework papers, often neglecting to bring them home, much less complete them. I asked her about the other times when Kenny would do things at home.

Mom: He'll do things, he just has to be 'made' to do them. He's really a sweet boy.

LM: I can tell. How do you get him to do things?

Mom: He has to know that I mean it.

I suggested to Mom and Kenny that he certainly had the ability to be a good student, mostly because when he knew that he was supposed to do things or when he liked something, he did it. I asked Mom (in front of Kenny) if she wouldn't mind going to school with Kenny once or twice next week, only to make sure that Kenny knew when he was supposed to turn in his homework and how to bring new homework assignments home. While Kenny disagreed of the necessity of Mom coming to school, I reassured him that Mom would only go when he forgot to turn in his homework. I asked Mom to ask his teacher to call her whenever he forgot, a message that she was needed the next day. When he did remember, I asked that the teachers compliment him.

Mom went to school with Kenny one time. The next time he came to my office, all eight dividers were full of assignments.

Fitting into the student's world view lessens resistance and encourages cooperation

Karen, a junior in high school, has lost interest in her history class. Her father came to a conference with Karen's teacher and said things in front of Karen that were quite hurtful. Apparently her father's high expectations were backfiring on him, encouraging rebellion in Karen, whose performance ability was a "B". Currently, she was in danger of failing history. Notice how a dire situation such as this one was helped by talking about Karen differently to her father, helping her father to relax his efforts.

Teacher: Karen, I've been looking back over the semester and I remembered some things about you during the beginning of the year that I wanted to tell your father. Mr. Smith, your daughter is one of the most talented students in my class. She has always been courteous to me and respectful. You should be quite proud of her. I guess we all get bored sometimes with things, and Karen has simply reached that point. I am interested in helping her to be interested again so that she can be the student that she has been for most of the semester ... a competent and successful one. She did that on her own.

Teacher: Karen, even though you are bored at the moment, I am still impressed that you are coming to class and listening so respectfully. How are you doing that?

Karen: I have to come. I want to graduate.

Teacher: Good reason.

Father: But she's almost failing.

Teacher: Mr. Smith, you are so helpful. I wonder, though, is your strategy of worrying and pushing Karen to do her work helping?

Father: I guess not ... that's why we're here talking.

Teacher: I would like to invite you to do something different then. I want you to watch for the successful student that Karen was at the beginning of the semester, just for a week. And Karen, do whatever it takes so that your father notices the kind of student you truly are inside ... so that you can graduate.

What happened in this brief dialogue? The teacher attempted to understand Karen as well as her father. It would have been easy to ask the father to "back off", but typically, parents whose expectations are high rarely want to do that. They seem to feel that pushing harder is the answer. By asking the father "is this *strategy* working", his negative reply gives the teacher an opportunity to suggest something different. Then the teacher paves the way for Karen to show her competency again, in an atmosphere where she would be the expert on her success. Karen began to bring up her grades and the teacher gave her all of the credit.

Motivation is a key and can be encouraged by aligning with students against the problem

What's different when we think of a *learning disabled student* and a student who is challenged by *learning difficulties*? Why does it sound more *hopeful* when we talk of a student who is bothered by *anger sometimes*, instead of talking about him as an angry student.

The difference is semantics. The problem-focused view can create the impression that the student is the problem. A solution-focused teacher subscribes to the belief that *the problem is the problem.*

A kindergarten teacher welcomed a five-year-old into her class early one spring morning. The student was accompanied by his mother who, frowning, shared that her son, Mike, had been to several private kindergartens, all of which had trouble with his temper tantrums. Now in a public school, she was worried that his tantrums would get him in trouble. She had already visited with the school counselor who promised to help the teacher. The kind and patient teacher assured the mother that things would be fine.

Within a few days the teacher was losing her patience. Mike had temper tantrums every morning around ten o'clock. While the school counselor helped, Mike often disrupted the class to the point of no return. She had been attending one of the solution-focused seminars I was doing at her school. One morning, after school started at eight o'clock, she took a different approach.

Teacher: Mike, do you know what time it is? It is 8:30. The big hand on the clock here has gone from the twelve to the six, that's thirty minutes. How have you kept the temper tantrum from bothering you?

Mike: Staring, speechless.

Teacher: Tell you what … let's see if you can go thirty more minutes … you know, until the big hand on the clock goes from six to twelve. Okay?

Mike: Okay. (Surprised, and still speechless.)

Thirty minutes later…

Teacher: Mike, my goodness … you have now gone over sixty minutes. That's thirty-six HUN-DRED seconds. You are so strong. Tell me, who are the Teenage Mutant Ninja Turtles' names on your T-shirt?

Mike: Rafael, Michaelangelo, Leonardo, and Donatello.

Teacher: Who is the strongest?

Mike: Michaelangelo. He's the strongest of all of them.

Teacher: Mike, you are stronger than Michaelangelo. You have kept the tantrum away for thirty-six hundred seconds. Can you keep it up?

Mike: Yes … I am strong.

Teacher: You really are. You are in control. You are strong. You have won over the temper tantrum. When the little hand gets to eleven and the big hand gets to the six, I will let you be the strong leader and take us to the bus.

Mike: Wow. Okay.

17

Mike's temper tantrums disappeared. Mike's mother called the teacher two weeks later to ask what was going on at school because her son was so happy.

There is no such thing as resistance when we cooperate

One of my favorite phrases to say to adolescents is:

"It is so sad that your teachers (or parents) misunderstand you. What do you think they are missing?"

I like this phrase because it melts resistance and sends the message that I am on the side of the adolescent. Adolescents love to feel as if their presence is important. Validation and acceptance are paramount to gaining the respect and cooperation of adolescents. The phrase is a compliment. Additional ways of using this phrase follow.

For a student who is failing a class:

"Looking over your grades, Sean, it occurs to me that on several occasions your grades were incredible. I wonder what that said about you as a student? I wonder how you might get back into that reputation?"

For a student complaining about another teacher:

"It's too bad that your homeroom teacher doesn't see you as I do. I know she runs her class differently, but can you tell me what you might do to show her that you can be a star student, like you are in my class?"

For a student who is talking back disrespectfully:

"Jake, I really want to get along with you today, like we have earlier this year. This is the first time you have talked negatively to me in class since the beginning of school three weeks ago. Tell me, what was going on in class then that kept you from getting upset? I am interested."

For a student who refuses to work in class:

No dialogue; chances are the student won't reply. Instead, consider cooperating with the student's lack of cooperation by giving a note to the student as she leaves the classroom:

Dear Susie, I remember at the beginning of the semester how helpful you were in answering some of the questions in our geometry class. You have such a gift in math. You showed me your ability six weeks ago and proved it by making a "B". I look forward to seeing you in action again in my classroom.

Come by early to my class tomorrow so that we can look at which papers you need to make up so that your grades will reflect what a good student you are. I look forward to talking to you.

Ms Johnson

If it works, don't fix it—if not, do something different

Across the nation, students are sent to in-school suspension programs and off-campus alternative schools. Looking into those particular "hot files" we see that the same students have been sent time and time again. One might deduce from such a discovery that the programs are not working since the same students attend over and over. Obviously the programs are not threats or the students wouldn't mind going. Instead, it is helpful to examine what it is about the alternative school environment that *does work*. The following comments were made by students attending such alternative campuses:

"The classes are structured and organized, and I have to do my work."

"The teachers are patient and understanding, yet you know you have to follow the rules."

"The classroom is quiet. I like it quiet. I don't talk to my friends so I do better."

It seems only fitting, then, that as a student returns from an alternative school setting, he or she be asked:

"What worked for you in _____ school that we should know about?"

Three exciting things happen when this question is asked:

1. The student is forced to become competent regarding his or her present success and the verbalization of such helpful elements in the alternative school setting helps teachers to see the student differently.

2. The student sees the faculty in his or her home school differently, as a group (all teachers should be present for this exercise to be most effective) of teachers who are interested in being the most helpful.

3. The negative atmosphere that surrounded the student when he or she was placed in the alternative setting dissipates into one that presumes that things will be different upon his or her return.

Focusing on the possible and changeable lessens frustration

In order for most problem-solving techniques to work, a goal must be generated. Solution-focused problem solving is no different. What *is* different is the way the goals are specifically stated, as if videotaping them was possible.

Observe the following nonspecific goals and why they are hard to attain:

"I want to do better in school."

"I want Joey to stop hitting me on the playground."

"If I could just be happier in school, things would be better."

"I want to make an A instead of failing Math like I always have."

"I need to remember to turn in my homework."

Each goal has a nice intent but little suggestion of what actions should be taken, leaving the student stranded with a goal that has little direction. Ben Furman, MD, suggests the following exercise for goal setting. This exercise can be used with parents as well as students.

1. Fold one piece of paper in half. On one side, list all of the problems that are currently bothering you (or your child) in school.

2. Open up the paper. Across from the problems, on the other side, write down what you think you should *do* or what you need to *do* in order to solve the problems.

3. Tear the page in half and toss away the problems. All that is left are the solutions. Concentrate on these as goals.

Another quick intervention for setting a goal is to ask a scaling question (De Shazer, 1985):

"How will you know when things are better for you in school?"

"On a scale of 1–10, with a '10' meaning that you have achieved that goal completely and a '1' meaning that you are far from achieving that goal, where are you now?"

(Draw the scale below.)

not successful   successful

_____

   1   2   3   4   5   6   7   8   9   10

"Where would you like to be by next week?"

"What will you be doing when you move up just half a point?"

Go slowly and focus on tasks that lead to success

Lasting change takes time, although it can and will happen *quickly* using a solution-focused approach. Throughout this book you will notice that students, teachers, and parents are asked to do something different for no longer than a week at a time. Why? Because it opens the door for greater success when someone is only asked to do it for a short time. Most of us can do something different for a short time. The important  aspect of the experience is that we enjoy it, encouraging us to do it again. The following are some guidelines for time allotments that can be used with different-aged students:

kindergarten: a morning or afternoon

grades 1–3: a day

grades 4–6: a day or two

grades 7–9: two or three days

grades 10–12: three days to a week

In addition, referring to the new actions as an "experiment" allows for failure or moratorium of the goal. An experiment does not have to succeed—nor does it fail. Should the goal not be accomplished, yet behaviors do not deteriorate, the teacher can simply say:

"Tell me how you have kept things from getting worse?"

Or,

"It's understandable that we didn't get it the first time. It was only an experiment. Tell me, what would you suggest doing that might make a difference just for a day?"

Rapid change is possible when we identify exceptions

What does geometry and football have in common for a sophomore in high school? How about parenting strategies for a father who teaches and manages a fifth-grade classroom? What if a surgeon used his bedside manner with his sixteen-year-old? What if an overwhelmed single mother used her organizational skills as a secretary at home with her third grader to give him some much-needed attention? Notice how the skills in one area can be used in another. These are referred to as "exceptions", or the times when the problem occurs less.

Exceptions will be discussed throughout this book, but for this guideline, the following example shows the competency that can happen when a geometry teacher focuses on exceptions outside of the classroom with a sophomore who can't remember when math was successful for him.

Teacher: Larry, you are a defensive player on our football team. In fact, you are one of our best players. I know that you have to remember plays.

Larry: All the time.

Teacher: How do you do that?

Larry: I can never remember them when the coach tells us. I have to go home and get poster board and draw them really big. Then I stare at them.

Teacher: That's great. So you learn best visually.

Larry: I guess.

Teacher: It seems that the only thing holding you back from doing better in geometry are the formulas. Since you memorize things well for football by drawing them, I wonder if the same strategy would help here.

Larry: I never thought about it . . . maybe so.

Change is constant

Perhaps the hardest aspect of becoming a solution-focused teacher is noticing when problems are not happening, then verbalizing when those good times happen to students and parents. Noticing when the problems happen is easy. Problems stand out because they interfere with our lesson plans, priorities, plans, or goals. It's more difficult to remember to comment on Shari's positive attitude when some of the other students in the class are not on task. However, watching for Shari's positive attitude and other students who *are* on task is vital for their continuance. Many students will continue no matter what. For those students "at risk" of losing their good attitude, it is essential to notice when change happens.

If Ms. Jordan had not noticed that Tom performed well with prompting, reminders and reviews, she might not have given him the chance to earn five points, enabling him to pass. Noticing when change happens is the quickest route to solutions.

Changing the time and the place will change interactions and behaviors

Students create bad reputations through their negative behaviors, reactions, and words. With this in mind, keeping the same context promotes more of the same. I recently visited with an adolescent male who had moved from one school district to another when his parents moved. When he came to talk to me the first time, he asked if I had heard of him. When I told him "no," he acted surprised. He said he had been in trouble so much in the previous district that he had his *own chair* in the vice principal's office. He had been in counseling for four years! He had moved from what I knew to be a conservative school district to a rather challenging one, full of gangs and violence.

His mother believed that he still needed help, yet I was more intrigued about his current success, since it was November and he had not had a single disciplinary infraction since school began in August.

LM: This is amazing to me. The school you attend has a real reputation for gangs, violence, and drugs. How are you managing to be so successful?

Vince (Looking at his mother, pointing to me ...): I don't know. No one has ever said that I was doing well in school. I have been going to counselors for four years.

LM: Really, let's think about it for a minute. What are you allowing these teachers to see that the other teachers didn't see?

Vince: I guess that I study? That I can do the work. I'm in all honors classes. Before, the other teachers would just say 'get out' when I said anything in class.

LM: What are you doing differently now?

Vince: I guess the teachers don't know me so they are nice to me. Before, every year when school started, even the new teachers threatened me without even knowing me. There were two teachers in the past four years who didn't yell at me. They seemed to understand me. I did fine in their classes.

It is not always possible to transfer students from one school to another, but almost the same effect can happen when teachers directly say to a challenging student:

"Vince, we have clashed in the past. Let's try, just for today, to work together. Tell me what I can do to help that to happen."

Looking at problems differently can encourage their resolutions

Remember Kenny, the twelve-year-old who had been bothered by ADHD all of his school life? As Kenny began to improve in his schoolwork, his mom and I discussed his home life as well. It seems that she had read all of the literature on ADHD and was quite cautious in her dealings with Kenny. However, her ex-husband was not quite so cautious and Kenny would always complete his chores on visitation, according to his dad. When Mom and I discussed how she viewed Kenny, she said she viewed him as "ADHD, challenging, impulsive, distractible, forgetful, and belligerent at times." The following dialogue then transpired:

LM: When you think of Kenny in this way, how do you react when he refuses to do his chores or get ready for school?

Mom: I am way too lenient, then I get frustrated, yell and MAKE him do it. People tell me I give him too much slack.

LM: We have talked about how Kenny will do things when he wants to because he likes the activity, like Band, and when he is made to do them, like when he has turned in his homework over the past week. If we came up with a new label or description for Kenny that was different from the pathological one you think of now, what would it be like?

Mom: He's spoiled.

LM: Okay, and how might you deal with him, thinking of him in that way, just for a week?

Mom: I would stay consistent, and expect him to do things before he visited his dad or went out to see friends.

When Mom returned two weeks later, she told me that not only did Kenny do better at home during that time, but she felt relieved, because she liked thinking of her son as more "normal" than as ADHD. Her new thinking seemed to give her more parenting options.

The following case is a nice conclusion to this chapter since it contains all of the components of being solution focused with a school problem. The case and the dialogue are all true, and appeared originally in my book Counseling Toward Solutions (The Center for Applied Research in Education, 1995). I was asked to consult on the case by the school.

Easing the tension: A case study

Joey, 15, a sophomore in high school, had been a star athlete for most of his school years. He had played baseball since preschool and had excelled at the sport until this year when he was dropped from the team for failing three classes. The school was concerned about Joey's failing grades and his tendency to engage in fights.

As I listened to Joey's parents, I watched him stare at the floor and sink deeper and deeper into the couch, as if succumbing to "the problem" and its claim on his life. The parents were very concerned and their concern was burying Joey, creating a sense of hopelessness. The last thing I needed to do was to help them create more of the same hopelessness by trying to probe or understand what was troubling Joey, thereby giving credence to the fact that there indeed was a terrible problem.

A few years ago, I might have examined educational assessment forms, cumulative folders, and test scores. I might have asked the parents about the consequences they were currently giving to Joey since he was failing three classes. I might have asked personal questions to the parents regarding their family life, searching for *reasons why this problem was occurring, yet keeping my boundaries as an educator*. In an attempt to get to the root of the problem, I might have looked for sequences in behaviors, interactional patterns that did not work.

Instead, as I met with Joey, I refocused and tried to think differently about the situation, looking for something different. I looked for *exceptions* to when the school problem occurred. I was more interested in searching for Joey's competencies rather than perpetuating the problem through probing for more understanding of what Joey was doing wrong. Besides, Joey already knew. By Joey's sad appearance, he obviously knew enough about the problem that had brought him to me. In fact, by this point, he seemed to be feeling that *he was the problem!*

It's been my experience as a teacher that adolescents are a unique population who respond with rebellion, resistance, and sadness when blamed or criticized. I was interested in Joey's opinion and solutions to his school problems, and knew that to gain his cooperation, I needed to align heavily with him against the problem. I knew he was competent in at least part of his educational history, because he had, in fact, succeeded in school up to this point. He was 15 and a sophomore. He had also succeeded in doing well at a sport. Most important, he had still come to school, interested in working out the problems. He just had no clue as to where to begin. In his school career, he had rarely failed a class. With these *exceptions* in mind and an assumption that Joey wanted things different, I began talking to him.

LM: How will you know when things are getting better for Joey?

Mom: Things will be better when I don't worry as much about Joey's grades, or his outbursts at school. I will receive fewer phone calls about Joey's behavior.

Dad: The 'tension' which seems to perpetuate the home will be less prevalent and I'll be able to stay off Joey's back.

Joey: I don't know, I guess school will be better and everybody (parents and school) will be off my back.

LM: Joey, take me back to a time when school was better, and the 'tension' Dad was talking about wasn't in control of your life.

Joey: Last year. I passed all my classes last year.

LM: How did you do that?

Joey: They have this class at school called 'academic opportunity,' where you go for help when you need it … I went when I needed to and I passed.

LM: Really! By the way, aren't you passing four classes now?

Joey: Yes.

LM: Tell me which ones …

Joey: Math, English, Home Economics, and Art.

LM: That's great … what's your secret to doing that?

Joey: I don't know … I do my work in class and just hand it in.

Joey brightened considerably and instantly became more verbal. He began to describe additional ways he had passed classes in the past and strategies he currently used to pass some of his classes. He recalled how, a few years ago, his mom praised him and rewarded him with time together. He also mentioned that she had been reacting differently lately, not noticing his passing grades and barely acknowledging any progress. Instead, she yelled and grounded him. According to Joey, Mom's efforts to encourage him had backfired.

Joey turned his attention to his stepdad and reminisced how he and his stepdad had previously gone over work together before he turned it in. Stepdad admitted that he had become negligent in checking Joey's work recently, and recalled that he did enjoy checking Joey's work in the past. As Joey described his past successes, Mom mentioned her concern about the violent outbursts at school. Joey admitted that he had a temper, but by this time in the session he too was changing his thinking as he mentioned that on more than one occasion since eighth grade, he had learned to curb his temper. I was curious about his ability to curb his temper, especially since that was an issue brought to my attention by his parents and school, and asked him to describe how he did that.

Joey: One day at school, I was sitting with six of my friends at lunch. We got up to go get food and when we came back a bunch of guys had thrown our books on the floor and were sitting in our seats. It took about 15 seconds for me to clench my fists and get ready to fight.

LM: Did you fight?

Joey: No.

LM: How did you stop?

Joey: We asked them would they please move … and then I noticed the coach watching us. I slowed myself down.

LM: Wow, you asked them to move first?

Joey: Yeah.

LM: Has being polite and calm helped you in other situations?

Joey: Yeah, it has.

LM: That's incredible … tell me.

It was very important that Joey experience himself as competent, so as to lessen any dependency on his parents and teachers to succeed in school, both behaviorally and academically. Gaining independence from the problem is, for adolescents, a self-esteem builder and motivating agent for change. By later saying to Joey to "notice when school works", I supposed that change would occur.

LM: Joey, during the next week, I'd like you to notice when school works, especially in the four classes you are passing, and watch specifically how you are doing that.

Within a week, Joey's stepdad again began checking Joey's work, and his mom stopped worrying and became more positive in her reactions to Joey. After three weeks, Joey raised his grades to passing. Interestingly enough, in a future meeting, Mom said to me that even she had changed. She said, "I started noticing what he passed instead of what he was not passing, and the times we got along instead of what went wrong that day." I was happy to give her credit for such a nice way of relating differently to her son, although I never asked her to change anything! Joey received all the credit for his academic improvements.

The ideas and questions that were used in Joey's situation were an example of using a *solution-focused way of thinking and conversing about a school problem*. The problem was discussed only as it was presented by the student and his parents. The goals of Joey's parents were defined by using the *language* of the family members and the school. If I had questioned the parents and hinted at any *dysfunction* on the part of Joey, his family,

or teachers, I would have run the risk of hearing blame for the problem. Instead, I asked for specific goals so I would be listening to what *Joey* wanted to accomplish. No insight was required.

In school, the student's system—which includes the student, his family, teachers, and peers—can maintain or dissolve school problems by their response to them. As in physics, when one part of a system changes, so does the entire system change. It is because of interactions within systems that problems are perceived and conceived. The use of different interactions, therefore, can encourage solutions by noticing and verbalizing how and when success occurred before—when the problem was absent. This change in behaviors and perception will not allow the problem to remain as such, since it changes all the rules of interaction, blame, and responsibility.

Concluding comments

The times have changed and so must our strategies. In Chapter One, a new approach has been explained. The following chapters will deal with specific conversational strategies and activities that will reinforce the ideas presented here. Such strategies will make the difference for you professionally, so that school enriches your life as well as your students. The following excerpt and dialogue from Northern Exposure, a popular television series several years ago, serves to end this chapter in an insightful way:

Ed, a Native American, watched Ira, a woodcarver, cut an Alder branch from a tree and begin to carve it into a flute.

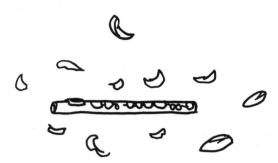

Ed: How do you know where to carve?

Ira: The branch will show me where to carve. See how the knife glides over the branch, like so? … Inside every Alder branch is a flute. Your job is to find it …

This week, watch for the flute.

Chapter One Practice Exercise
Thinking with a Solution Focus

Think of a student whose behaviors are currently frustrating you and disturbing your classroom. On the left side, under the word *Problem*, write down all of the problems *you* are currently experiencing as a result of this student's misbehavior.

On the right, under the word *Solutions*, write down what you would see the student doing when the problem is resolved. Keep the solutions behavioral and literal.

Problem	**Solutions**
Example:	
Karen talks and interrupts me when I am beginning the lesson.	Karen would not be interrupting me. She should know when it is time to talk.

_____

_____

_____

_____

_____

After you have listed the problems and the solutions, fold this paper in half. Focus only on the solutions that you wrote down. Think of your past strategies with the student. Eliminate those that did not work. Think of those that worked slightly. Now think of some *solution-focused* strategies that were discussed in Chapter One and, just for the next week, *do something different to accomplish your solutions*.

A Solution-Focused Guide for Helping Students and Parents

This is a *brainstorming sheet* to use as a guide when you are helping a student or parents with a school or personal issue. Below, list the problem, the goal of the student or parents, and the exceptions or times when the problem occurs less. Finally, write down new strategies as tasks for the student or parent.

Problem (according to student or parent):

_____

_____

Goal (according to the student or parent, stated in behavioral, specific terms):

_____

_____

Exceptions (times now or in the past when the problem occurred less):

1. _____

2. _____

3. _____

4. _____

5. _____

Task (new strategies developed from exceptions):

1. _____

2. _____

3. _____

_____   _____
Teacher signature   Student/Parent signature

Chapter Two
Creating Possibilities for Student Success Through Language

"If in our world language plays a very central part in those activities that define and construct persons, the redescription of persons is called for."

—*Narrative Means to Therapeutic Ends*, David Epston and Michael White

Mr. Clark dreaded the parent conference with Ms. Yu that afternoon. For days he had rehearsed the statements he would make about Philip's academic failure and had brainstormed different ways of talking to Philip's mother so that he would appear empathetic, positive, and professional. His fellow teachers had consoled and warned him to stand his ground or Ms. Yu, they said, would "eat you alive"! Forewarned, Mr. Clark approached the conference room where Ms. Yu sat, already defensive, it seemed, ignoring his greeting and his outstretched hand. He began the conference by opening his grade book, and speaking calmly to Ms. Yu.

Mr. Clark: I want you to know first and foremost that I enjoy having Philip in my classroom. I rarely have to correct him and he seems quite polite. However, Ms. Yu, it seems that Philip has problems turning in his homework on time. He also seems to have difficulty memorizing the definitions I assign in class. He seems to be an average student, yet he does not catch on as quickly as some of the other students. I have certain material to cover in my class and sometimes I have to move on even if Philip hasn't grasped the ideas completely. I'm sure you understand. At times he seems to be daydreaming and loses his place, particularly when we are reading a chapter out loud. I'm concerned about his success here at school.

I would like to offer Philip tutoring after school, three days a week. He can come into my classroom and for thirty minutes I will review the previous day's work and help him with whatever he needs. This way if he misses something we discuss in class, he can catch up. If there's anything you can do to encourage him to do his homework and turn it in, that would be very helpful.

Silence. Then it happened, just like his colleagues had warned. Ms. Yu exploded!

Ms. Yu: How dare you assume that my son can't learn. He has always had mild difficulty with memorizing terms, but he can do it. He's passed other classes where memorizing was important. How can you sit there so smug, and describe to me all of the things that are wrong with my child. Why, and to offer tutoring to him when I, myself, am a teacher? How dare you! Don't you realize that I should be the one doing the tutoring? I am insulted. Where is your principal? How can he allow such insulting behavior at his school by one of his teachers! This happened last year with Ms. Kinsey. You all think you know exactly what's wrong with my little boy. Well, you are not going to treat him this way.

This dialogue is from a true story, relayed to me by a principal of an elementary school. What productivity happened in this conversation between a sincere teacher and a

concerned, yet defensive parent? Nothing. Mr. Clark's descriptions of what was *wrong* with Philip were ample and he even took time to compliment Philip as a polite and enjoyable student. Yet his problem focus soon took over and sent a message to Ms. Yu that *Philip couldn't learn as well as the other students*. Even worse, he attempted to give solutions without consulting the person in need of help and his mother. Ms. Yu responded to the problem focus with threats and blaming. No one accomplished anything. As far as Ms. Yu was concerned, the problem was with her son's teacher, not with her son.

Changing the outcome by changing the conversation

Consider how the following alternative solution-focused conversation could have been created by Mr. Clark. Suppose that Mr. Clark began to think differently about Philip, using a different focus. Suppose he went looking for abilities and competency in certain classroom settings and situations instead of what Philip's problems were. He might have noticed the following competencies, as relayed to me by another of Philip's teachers:

- Philip learns best when he is closest to the teacher's desk. This seems to enable the teacher to prompt Philip often.
- When Philip is told before a lesson begins that he will be called on to read aloud, he pays closer attention, resulting in more productive assignments afterward.
- When Philip is asked for his homework assignments before leaving the classroom, Philip seems to remember to turn in the assignments, helping him to learn a responsible habit through repetition and routine.
- When Philip is reviewed orally with the class before a test, his long-term memory is refreshed and he performs better.

With these thoughts and observations in mind, Mr. Clark might have started the conference differently:

Mr. Clark: Ms. Yu, I want to say first and foremost how much I enjoy your son in my class. Last week, I asked the class for volunteers to take care of two gerbls in our class and your son's hand went up first. Did you know he was that responsible?

You know, when I looked at Philip's grades this morning in preparation for our conference, I noticed something very interesting. He makes passing grades on his tests when we review thirty minutes before the test. That observation has taught me to start doing it regularly! Then, I also noticed that he gets most of the definitions correct when I write them on the blackboard for the class to copy instead of just reading them out loud. He also does better when I stand next to him and remind him that I might be calling on him to read. He seems less distracted, too, in the past few days, since I have moved his desk nearer to mine. I have been reminding him to turn in his homework after he has a chance to finish it in class as well, and that seems to really be helping

him to remember. This afternoon he remembered before I said anything. These are the things I have noticed about Philip. I've made a copy of these observations for you to take with you.

I know that you requested this conference, Ms. Yu. Can you tell me what you are expecting from Philip and from me here at school? I am interested in your ideas and your suggestions.

How is Ms. Yu likely to respond to such a productive array of observations? Differently. In the solution-focused dialogue, Mr. Clark appears to have done *his* homework on Philip. Chances are, Ms. Yu will have little to become defensive about in this solution-focused conversation. It is more likely that Ms. Yu will perceive that her son's teacher is on Philip's side and will be more cooperative with Mr. Clark instead of blaming him for her son's failure. The conference would probably be respectful and would encourage Ms. Yu's input and ideas for solutions. Mr. Clark would give Philip's mom an opportunity to see that her son could succeed with the proper context, promoting hope and motivation in the parent to assist her son. When a teacher creates such a context for a parent, he creates an opportunity for both student and parent to participate and assist him in being the most effective educator he can be. *If* the teacher takes on full responsibility for changing the educational direction without consulting the student or parents, he may miss out on information that could benefit everyone and set himself up for confrontations if his direction does not work. It seems fairer to share the responsibility and the success with everyone involved.

The student–teacher–parent relationship: the most powerful tool of all

Chapter Two focuses on ways to create new possibilities for student success through new ways of thinking about and reacting to students, parents, and colleagues. This is a tremendous task, one that can take its toll on the best of educators. Today's students and their parents are very different from those of ten or twenty years ago, yet their need to be respected, accepted, and nurtured is the same as it always has been. In addition, the need of a challenging parent to see his or her child as successful and respected is great, too, for without any possibility of hope, some parents give up and their children lose important support. Obviously, some student behaviors and academic performances do not always encourage teachers to give students nurturing and acceptance. It is certainly heartbreaking to be cursed at or threatened when one works hard to be an effective teacher in the classroom. Teachers do not deserve that. They work hard for their students and deserve an atmosphere where they feel competent and respected by their students as well. Unfortunately, it is still the teachers who must begin to create such an environment even when the difficulties are immeasurable. Students are the first to notice a teacher who cares more about the rules and is inflexible with expectations *and* they are the first to say "she likes what she does" or "she's nice to us … she likes us," about their teachers. Teachers who earn descriptions such as these conduct the collaborative, cooperative classrooms that are most easily transformed into solution-

focused classrooms. The absence of such a respectful relationship affects student performance, influences behavior, and, even worse, models negative interactions for students, even when the teacher has the best of intentions.

Creating possibilities for troubled students is very difficult and at first may not be responded to with enthusiasm from the student. Don't give up! Chances are the troubled student has been faced with trials and tribulations that you could only imagine. The student may be conditioned to become defensive even when you are being kind and considerate. Realize that he or she comes from a different place than you do. Also, just because a student or parent might not comply at first to new ideas or your new descriptions, try not to assume that they are not interested in changing. Persevere and you will make a difference! The fact that they are present to have the conversation means they care at least a little about the situation at hand. That is an exception. Chances are that the student or parent simply may not know how to be productive at the moment and are relying on the teacher for answers, even if the answers given to them are not accepted. It is *this* situation in which the solution-focused approach can be the most successful because it is so respectful! Imagine feeling helpless and hopeless, but a teacher—with four or more years of college—commends your efforts and your past success with your child, even when you don't see any success at all in your life or your child's! In my experiences as a teacher and therapist, I have yet to meet a parent who felt worse when I pointed out his or her strengths. By involving the parent in developing solutions and listening to the exceptions the parent and students uncover that have worked before, the teacher assists everyone in altering the student's *system* and creates a possibility that success is imminent.

Buying into the freedom of solution talk

The way Mr. Clark thought about Philip influenced how he talked to Philip's mother. It is easy to see problems and think of students with *problem talk* phrases such as "learning differenced, lazy, ADD, a dreamer, uninterested, loser, …" Yet when we think of the same students using *solution talk* we create more options for everyone, including the student! Consider the difference in language in the following table. The first column describes actions with *problem talk* descriptions; the second column describes actions with *solution talk* descriptions. As you read them, think of how you might react as you think of students in both ways.

Problem Talk	Solution Talk
hyperactive	energetic
anxious/worried	tries to do things perfectly
shy	cautious
depressed	sad
temper tantrums	out of sorts
learning disabled	learns differently
emotionally disturbed	has difficulties coping at times
special education student	needs extra attention in school
reads below grade level	not yet at grade level
belligerent	opinionated
defensive	self-protective
disrespectful	inexperienced at gaining respect
lazy	not motivated, yet
disruptive	needs attention individually

The *solution talk* descriptions do not change or minimize the serious nature of any situation. Instead, the descriptions give teachers a chance to gain a new perception so that their interventions are *different*, solution focused, and thereby more effective. This is a difficult process to adopt, for the world operates on problem talk. What seems helpful is to consider how the *problem talk* keeps **you** stuck. For example, if a teacher is presented with a new student labeled learning differenced and ADHD, she will probably predict to herself that there will be difficulties in teaching the student. If a parent presents a kindergartner to a teacher on the first day, describing in detail all of the difficulties he had in the previous kindergarten that expelled him, the teacher is likely to *expect* challenges and notice them readily. Assuming outcomes is unfair to both teacher and student since it restricts our interventions and our vision for the student. Learning to ignore assumptions and looking through eyes that see competence in spite of the mask of misbehavior and failure can be a teacher's greatest asset.

In the following case study, a young teacher learns firsthand how a simple change of thinking enhances her class management skills, encourages student motivation, and relaxes the atmosphere in her classroom. As you read it, recall a student you might have been frustrated with and see if Sarah's strategies sound familiar.

This student is impossible! A case study

Sarah, an English teacher, complained of a ninth-grade student who continuously disrupted her sixth-period class by making jokes about the readings from *Romeo and Juliet*. He would come into class and disrupt her introduction, talking out loud and interrupting her. The other students seemed to like the student so they paid more attention to him than to Sarah. I asked Sarah how she was thinking about the student, and then asked her to describe for our teacher supervision class how she reacted when she thought of him in those ways. Her descriptions are in the first column. Her reactions are in the column to the right.

Description of Student Behavior	Teacher's Reaction
disrespectful	"I give him consequences,
belligerent	correct him constantly, and
uncooperative	threaten to send him to the
disruptive	principal. He does not listen."
defiant	
impossible	

When I asked Sarah if her strategies were working, she quickly said, "No!" I asked the class to help Sarah come up with some *redescriptions* of the same student and then to think of how they might react to the same situation while thinking of him differently (White & Epston, 1990). The following are their suggestions.

Redescription	Teacher's Reaction
creative	"Let him choose certain lines to read and
class clown	ask him to interpret them for the class in
high energy	a humorous way. Let him read first. Ask
bored	him to pass out papers/rearrange the
	room after the readings."

Sarah was slightly reluctant because she was so frustrated with the student, but was also desperate enough to try to think of him *differently* for only the next week. It was difficult for her to think she *had* to change first when the student was causing her so much stress. However, thinking of the student as being *inexperienced in the world* and in need of her cooperation to help him "conform" seemed to help Sarah take the risk. When she returned to our class a week later, she remarked with excitement how much *the student* had changed! When we asked her specifically what she had done differently in class, she replied:

"I gave him more lines to read from the play and I always let him read first. When I noticed that he seemed to like getting the attention, I gave more attention to him and told him outside of class that he did a good job. Each

day when he came into the class I invited him to tell a joke or share something with the class to start off our time. Eventually he talked less and definitely participated in a more polite way."

From that point on, Sarah's semester went smoothly, was less stressful, and her student's grades improved along with his cooperation. I asked Sarah to continue watching for days when the student did well in her class, and asked her to specifically watch for what she was doing that helped to promote those good days. Sarah learned indirectly to become flexible and cooperative with a disruptive student. Her old approach had not worked and she was in need of a new direction. When she redescribed her student differently, she opened doors to cooperation, even though it seemed unorthodox to do so. The results were worth it, however, when she saw changes occur almost immediately with her student's behavior and motivation.

Suggestions for helping students and parents to change negative assumptions

The attitude and perspective of the solution-focused teacher when working with students, parents, and colleagues is vital to the process of discovering and promoting student success. Students and parents in conflict tend to see only what is not working at school. If the focus stays on the complaints, the possibilities for solution diminishes, people blame other people, and the student is left with little direction except for tried-and-true methods that may or may not work. In the following case, a parent is assisted by the teacher to look at her own competencies as a parent to help her son with a school problem.

Mom, give me a break! A case study

The following dialogue occurred between a teacher and the mother of a ten-year-old elementary student who was having problems turning in his homework assignments on a regular basis. The teacher had previously given Ken's mom some information regarding how important it was for Ken to do his homework and some suggestions for how she could help Ken do his homework at home. When the ideas did not completely work, the teacher took a new direction and placed the responsibility back on Ken and his mom for solutions.

Parent: I just do not know what to do with Ken. He says that he does his homework, yet he will not turn it in. I have tried everything but he continues to defy me at home with temper tantrums and downright refusing to do his homework when I tell him to. It's such a battle. This morning was just terrible. He had forgotten to do part of his homework yesterday afternoon and I became very upset and yelled at him. I felt horrible when I dropped him off at school. Sometimes I feel like I should just let him fail but I really don't want that to happen. He's always required some pushing on my part but not like this.

Teacher: I'll bet you are frustrated. You seem to be the kind of parent who really puts forward a lot of effort in encouraging him. No wonder you are upset. Tell me, when is it that Ken responds better to doing the things you need him to do? Do confrontations like you had this morning before school help or has something else been more effective in the past?

Parent: Well, obviously confrontations do not help. They make me feel bad and they make him even more defiant. When he was younger I could talk to him in a calm way and give him incentives or rewards, but this year he has become more defiant and all I think I can do is to punish him.

Teacher: So it sounds as if punishments aren't working either. Tell me more about the incentives that you used to give him.

Parent: Last year I rewarded him for keeping his grades above 80 by taking him to a miniature golf center or to play video games on Saturday mornings. The teacher would send a note home each Friday that would list his average. That worked pretty well until this year. Now when he comes home, all he wants to do is play soccer until dark in the park down the street. I want him to do his homework as soon as he comes in so that he gets it over with but he complains that all of his friends are going to the park. That's when the trouble starts.

Teacher: So that strategy of getting him to do homework immediately after school doesn't work this year.

Parent: Right.

Teacher: Maybe we should think of Ken as a student who needs to take a break from school work in the afternoon instead of just being defiant. Sounds like he's growing up and his friends are becoming very important. I've noticed, too, that he likes to work for extra points in class, so it sounds like incentives still work with him. I wonder how you might approach him if you used an incentive again, especially since he seems to enjoy soccer this year instead of miniature golf.

Parent: Well, maybe he could go play soccer after school when I knew he turned in all of his homework that day. That would mean that he would have to bring home a note or some sort of assignment sheet again. I thought we were past that but it did work last year. Would you mind signing or initialing a sheet of some sort when he turned in his work?

Teacher: Sure. Why don't you draw one up and send it to school with Ken tomorrow.

Notice how the parent dropped the expectation that the teacher *do something* and began thinking back to times when Ken responded slightly better to her. The parent knew her son better than anyone else but she must have felt that understanding how to solve Ken's school problems was too difficult for her level of expertise. The solution-focused teacher helped her to feel competent by reminiscing back to times when the student was more productive. The parent knew the likes and dislikes of her son, his

responses to incentives, and his tendency to rebel at punishment. When the teacher empathized with her and shared her frustration, the parent was able to see that she could take care of the situation herself. When parents sense that teachers and administrators see them as competent, they are more likely to pursue the challenge more effectively and confidently. When teachers or administrators take full responsibility and tell parents how to fix the situation, the following often happens:

1. Parents assume educators know better than they do how to help their children and will most likely expect the educators to solve other future problems for them instead of devising new strategies themselves. In other words, the parents become less competent than the educators.

2. If the strategies given to the parents by the educators do not work, the parents can assume that even the school can't help their children so the situation must indeed be hopeless until their children decide to change. Thereafter, the students might slip into an unsuccessful and unmotivated role in which they feel no one is really interested.

3. If the strategies devised by the educators are not well received by the students or do not fit with the students' needs, the students may continue to respond negatively. At this point, everyone's goal for the students may overwhelm them and stifle their motivation altogether. When the students sense that strategies are being done to them rather than with them, they may not respond at all.

Ideas for changing negative assumptions

The following suggestions are ideas that the teacher in the previous case study considered in order to help the student and his parent to envision how school could change and improve. Notice how each suggestion respectfully acknowledges the past and the concerns of those involved, yet helps parent and student to focus on possibilities through the use of new words or stories.

1. Talk about the experiences as if they were in the past, available for reference, but also workable enough for redesigning in the future.

   "Sue, I certainly understand how moving four times in the past two years has made it difficult for you to feel as if you are a part of our school. Since I hear this so clearly from you, I wonder how you might like things to be different now that you know you will be at this school for the next full year, at least."

2. Encourage and invite very young children to imagine describing their story to a child in need of a solution. Help change their negative experience into a successful triumph over their problem (suggested by Keeney, 1994).

41

"Alex, I often teach children such as yourself who are very angry at a friend who did not treat them nicely. You have just told me that you want your school day to be happier. I'd like you to tell me in your own words what I might tell the next child who gets angry in my classroom. What would you tell that student to do?"

3. Redescribe behaviors that sound problem-focused into behaviors that seem more solution-focused.

"Kay, you seem to get upset when others tell you what to do. Gee, it sounds like you've got your own ideas, and people aren't listening to you like they should be. That seems to happen to many students. How would you like us to see you, as an angry student who closes her mind or as a creative student, like I see now, who has questions and suggestions about assignments? How might you do that just for this class period?"

4. Normalize behaviors for the student, teacher, or parent. Help them feel as if their situation occurs commonly and that they do not have a severe problem.

"Ann, I am really impressed that you have stayed in my geometry class this year. Many students wouldn't have forced themselves to go to tutoring, or persevere like you have. Even though your grade is low, you keep on going. How do you manage such drive to finish this class? What can I do to assist you?"

5. Present the idea to the student or parent that the current school story is in need of revision. They will probably agree! Help them to change the characters, interactions, and behaviors into a new scene in which the student does things differently. Do this by directly asking the student or parent how his or her peers, teachers, or parents would know that things were different.

"John, until now, things have been tough for you since you were placed in alternative school. People thought of you before as someone who was not serious about school and who often got off track and into trouble. Let's say that was 'Act One' in your life. How do you want 'Act Two' to go, now that you are back and have the chance to change their minds about you? I see something in you that the others haven't seen yet. Together, let's talk about how you can change the minds of others in 'Act Two'. What could you do, just for today that would start a new story?'

6. Assume change will occur or has already occurred.

"Lauren, someday soon when you are not so sad about your grandfather's death, what will you be doing more of? What small part of that could you do this afternoon?"

"Jonathan, when you bring your grades back up to passing during the next few weeks or so, what do you think will be different for you here at school and at home?"

"Ms. Juarez, when Rita begins to comply with your rules at home, using the ideas you and I have talked about here this morning, what do you see happening more often at home in your relationship with your daughter? I wonder what small thing you could do with or for her at the first glimpse that she is trying more?" (To Rita: "Do whatever it takes so your mom begins to notice!")

42

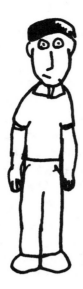  

7. Take time to notice when a student changes. Verbalize your observation to them or write a note to them or their parents.

    Karen, you paid attention to my instructions this morning and I watched how you completed the vocabulary words before you began talking to Sarah. I know that it was tempting to you to talk earlier, but you didn't. I just wanted you to know that I noticed. Would you take this note home to your dad? I wrote him a note about how you were so attentive today."

If you find that your thoughts about students keep you stuck, make you feel helpless, and even exhaust you, perhaps it's time to think differently, as an experiment. To see how your thoughts and assumptions can inhibit your creativity and stifle your willingness to try something different with troubled students, an exercise is provided entitled "Description, Perception … Action!"

Description, Perception ... Action!
Lee's Story – An Exercise

Lee, age 15, had been late to class to often and had accumulated 40 days in lunch detention as a result. A student who described himself as being down in the dumps fairly regularly, he looked forward to seeing his friends at lunch and often skipped lunch detention to the frustration of his vice principal. When Lee's detention days exceeded 45, he was sent to an alternative program for a week. His teachers were aware of his placement in the alternative setting and wondered how it would affect his motivation to be on time to class when he returned. Most of his teachers saw Lee as an "at-risk" student due to the crowd he hung around with, yet he passed all of his subjects the entire year. He was a quiet student and often looked very sad. At a parent–teacher conference once, they learned that his parents were divorced and that he had not seen his father for over five years. before Lee's older brother moved out two years ago, he often started fights with Lee at home and stole some of his possessions. Over the past year, Lee had become explosive at home when he became stressed with school or relationships, particularly with his girlfriend, who would break up with him and reconcile repeatedly. While Lee held many grudges against those who had hurt him, he played soccer for the high school team and hoped that he could attend college one day. When contacted by the vice principal, Lee's mother appeared very concerned about his violent outbursts but described him as a basically good person. She said that he helped her around the house, often without asking, went to church with her, and did not drink or do drugs. She is currently worried that his behavior at school will soon worsen since he is so upset with the vice principal and that he will drop out since school seems to have little meaning or be of much interest to him.

The Problem-Focused Approach

Under the words *Description of Problem*, write down all of the problems you recognized while reading Lee's story. Under the words *Perception of Outcome*, list what you perceive might happen if Lee continues to stay off track at school. Remember Lee's goal: to attend college. Under the word *Action*, write down how you might respond to Lee, utilizing the problem-focused *description* and *perception* that you wrote down in the first two columns.

Description of Problem	Perception of Outcome	Action

The Solution-Focused Approach

Under the words *Redescription of Resources*, write down the resources and strengths that you identified from Lee's story. Under the words *Perception of Success*, write down how the resources could assist Lee in getting back on track with school. Under the word *Action*, write down strategies you might begin to use with Lee as one of his teachers so that he gets back on track and make it to college.

Lee's Story–An Exercise *(continued)*

Redescription of Resources	Perception of Success	Action
_____	_____	_____
_____	_____	_____
_____	_____	_____
_____	_____	_____

Which approach seemed to promote student competency' the problem-focused or solution-focused actions?

_____

_____

What was it about those actions that were helpful?

_____

_____

Are your class management skills problem focused or solution focused? If you are an education student, which approach makes sense to you in the future?

_____

_____

If you are problem-focused, what can you do—just for tomorrow—to become more solution focused with *one* of your students?

_____

_____

What would that student see you doing differently that would tell him or her you were reacting differently?

_____

_____

_____

Did you have difficulty in identifying resources and strengths of Lee? Most educators do have difficulty at first looking beyond the problem and into competencies. Behaviors, attitude, and academic failure can easily mask the competencies of our students. What is helpful to remember is that focusing only on the problems does not help us to discover solutions. For example, if I know that a student has a problem with anger on the playground and that anger might be the result of his parents' divorce six months ago, I may have an understanding, yet I have no solutions. However, if I watch that student closely and search for times when the anger is not so prevalent, I might discover that when he receives one-on-one attention from me in the classroom or when he is working with a calm, mild-mannered classmate, he is not so angry. These discoveries can not only help me as his teacher, but I can relay the information to other colleagues as well.

What is the difference that makes the difference?

Walk down the hall in a school anywhere and you will see classrooms where students are on task and respectful and other classrooms where disruptions prevent teaching of any kind. What is the difference that makes the difference? The teacher's thinking, which translates into his or her actions—and the reactions of his or her students. Many students do not know how to express what their needs are so they get them met temporarily in negative ways. Teachers who see only problems respond negatively, which continues the cycle. Problem-focused strategies dominate today's classrooms and administration offices creating *more of the same* problems. Sadly, such behaviors are *learned* and internalized by students who return the favor back to their well-meaning teachers. This does not mean teachers should take abuse, however; it does mean they should see beyond the abusive tactics of students as unacceptable and show them how to respond through new modeling.

Teachers who see past the problems and seek student competency instead during the times when there are fewer problems, find that class management is easier. They seem to extinguish problems quicker because the students are less defensive. It's not that those teachers are simply positive; they show respect to their students even when they begin to be disrespectful. They stop thinking that the "student will get away with something if I back down"; instead, they do something different to extinguish the conflict. The teacher is concerned enough about a student's grade to give him or her a break or a special assignment. The message that these teachers relay is "I am here to work for you." This dynamic reminds me of a quote that applies well to today's schools:

> *"I've been waiting for twenty years for someone to say to me: 'You have to fight fire with fire' so that I could reply, 'That's funny—I always use water.' "*

Howard Gossage

Obviously there are more factors than simply school problems that cause students to act out, such as a difficult family situation, but there is always the possibility that modeling a new example of relating to others can grow into new actions. A teacher who is flexible and solution focused may be the only adult in a student's life who finds something to respect about him or her. When I present these ideas to teachers, I often get responses such as the following from teachers who try to make a difference in their students' lives:

"When there are so many problems at home, I can't really do much."

"What do you do when there is no parental cooperation and the teenager has little to no supervision or support to do his homework?"

"I am only one person . . . I can't be their parents too."

The teacher is only one person, true. Yet he or she may be the one person who can make the difference in a student's life … for a lifetime. The following excerpt from *Mentors, Masters and Mrs. MacGregor* will share how important a teacher's role can be:

> The day after 323 students graduated from our local high school, I learned one reason why my friend, Janet, received the newly-established, student-determined Teacher of the Year Award. My friend and I had decided to celebrate the end of the school year with a shopping and lunch outing. As we walked along the mall, she suddenly said, "Wait a minute, I just want to pop in this store to see if one of my students is still working here." As I entered the store, I saw my friend and a young girl deep in conversation. They stopped long enough for introductions. Then teasingly, I asked the student, "Oh, were you one of the seniors corrupted by Mrs. Cutler?" The girl became very serious, tears surfaced to her eyes. And she looked right at me and said, "Actually, Mrs. Cutler saved my life."
>
> As we left the store I asked, "What was that all about?" Janet replied, "Kim was having some huge family problems: Mother an alcoholic, Dad gone, boyfriend giving her a hard time. She had been absent the total number of days allowed by the school district. If she was absent one more day she would not graduate. So Kim and I made an agreement. I would call her every morning for the remaining eleven mornings and harass her, and she would come to school. One day it took four phone calls. But she made it and graduated. (Bluestein, 1995, pp. 169–170.)

Was it Ms. Cutler's phone calls or was it her intense interest in her student that motivated Kim to succeed? Only Kim knows the real answer but we can be assured that her teacher did something that her other teachers did not do … she took the time and never stopped trying to reach her.

Here's how one person made a difference in another student's life … *Someone* had to help Lee's transition back into school and that someone was me. When Lee (remember "Lee's Story"?) returned to school after his week in alternative school, I went with him to return for his first day back in school. I was interested in meeting the vice principal who Lee had described to me as "being on my case constantly . . . he sees me as trouble". I wanted Lee to feel more competent and I thought that he would have a better chance of succeeding at that when he changed his reputation at school. I sensed this because our conversation during his week in alternative school took a whole new direction when I began to compliment him on his success during that week. He told me he liked the teachers in his alternative school setting because they took a personal interest in him. His high school contained over 3,500 students and it was hard for his teachers to take time to talk to him. He also brightened up when I complimented him on listening to his mother and doing the chores she asked him to do without complaining. When he said he often felt "depressed", I mentioned that being "down" happened when life got off track and that he sounded very normal. I was impressed that he never let the "dumps" intrude on his school work so that he failed a subject or caused him to become violent at school. Talking over his competencies, Lee began to think differently about himself and when he left my office, he said, "You know, maybe it's not depression, maybe I just get bored."

As I talked with Lee's vice principal on his first day back at school, I asked him if he would watch closely over Lee during the next few weeks and notice what was different about him that meant that he had gotten back on track. I then asked Lee in the vice principal's presence to show those new behaviors in a bold way so that his vice principal would see him differently. The conversation seemed to serve as an icebreaker and Lee seemed to relax and feel more confident as we left the vice principal's office. Maybe he seemed happier because he no longer had lunch detention … the alternative school program erased those. Or maybe it was the first time he had ever talked to his vice principal for something not related to misbehavior. I may never know. But I do know that he was the only student smiling in the vice principal's office that day.

Those exceptional times

Up to this point, noticing times when students were less troubled by problems or were problem-free has merely been a suggestion to assist you in seeing them differently and encouraging a new reaction on your part. This suggestion is more than a strategy—it is the core theory of this book. Looking for *exceptions* gives teachers a new *direction*. When teachers have tried consequences, rewards, and praise to no avail, a change of direction that focuses on when the problem does not occur can lead to surprising solutions. Throughout the remainder of this book, the word *exception* will stand for "less problematic times" when a student's behavior is *slightly* different. The following are ideas and questions for teachers to consider when attempting to uncover exceptions.

Questions that focus on present exceptions

"Take me back to a time when school worked, even if it was a few days ago, a week ago, last year, or even years ago. What was different then? What went on in the classroom that made a difference for you? What else?"

"It seems like this year has been quite challenging. Can you think of times during this year when you felt school was more under your control? What was different on those days in the classroom? What did you do that helped? What did I do as your teacher?"

"I noticed that you did not get into a fight with Bill this afternoon at recess. How did you do that?"

"Sid, I am so impressed with your biology test. How would you explain the way you were able to pass this difficult test with an 80? How can we repeat this next week?"

"Joey, you have sat in your chair for ten long minutes this morning during our story time. How did you do that? I know it is tough for a young man like you with so much energy."

"When you memorize your football plays, what do you do that seems to work so well? I wonder how that might work with your geometry formulas?"

"Let's suppose that a miracle happened when you went to sleep tonight and you awoke tomorrow to find that your school life was much better. What would be different at school? How would that be helpful to you?"

Exceptions exist in all of our lives, yet they go unnoticed in comparison to the problems or interruptions that occur each day. Those are too bold to ignore! For example, think of the intrusions you might have experienced last week that kept your stress level high. Probably, they come to mind rather rapidly. Now consider the week's *exceptions*, or the ways that you lowered the level of stress that you felt. How did you encourage or help this happen? When you focus on those times when life works, you learn new actions or thoughts that can help your life to continue working. The same happens with students and parents when you point out the times when a student is *slightly successful* in some activity or lesson at school. Taking ideas from one situation and applying them to another seems simple. The tough part is identifying the situations that work. Sometimes stepping out of the situation and learning how students avoid the *situation* can give us clues. The following material will give ideas for seeing problems in a whole new way.

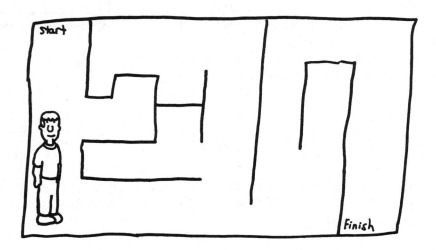

Externalizing problems to find the way out

Michael White (1989) talks of "externalizing" problems as a way to objectify or personify problems that intrude in our lives. If we think of ourselves as people whose lives are intruded upon by problems, we begin to look for ways around the problem to get back on track. Even better, we cease seeing ourselves as problematic and instead see the problem as the problem. As White began working primarily with ill children, he started to externalize the problem as an entity in itself that could either be maintained or dissolved. As he offered this suggestion for families, the families felt empowered and decided to eliminate the power of the problem over their lives by involving themselves in actions that stopped maintaining its influences on their lives.

Externalizing problems with adolescents and children also helps them to see problems as separate from themselves and to stop seeing themselves as failures. A young elementary boy might talk about his "energy" as something that keeps getting him in trouble. The teacher who talks to him in this way can suggest that he escape from the energy for fifteen minutes and become bigger than his energy. As he succeeds, no matter how many minutes he stays in control, the teacher can act amazed and say:

"Joey, can you believe that you were stronger than the energy for eight minutes? Wow."

Joey may not have made his goal of fifteen minutes, but staying stronger than the energy for eight minutes may motivate him to finish the last seven minutes.

A teacher could converse with a teenager who struggles with a habit of talking too often in class in this way:

"Melissa, I know how hard it must be when you let your talking keep you from listening to the history lesson. Is there a place in the classroom where you could sit today so that the talking doesn't take over?"

Melissa might not have recognized that she could be seen as a student whose talking gets in the way of her studying versus just being a talkative student. However, the teacher still made her point in a respectful manner and chances are Melissa might suggest another place to sit.

When teachers help students and parents to externalize problems, they also help them to see how their actions help to maintain the problem's existence. This creates an acute awareness of their responsibility in keeping the problem alive in their lives. In addition, it also frees them up to imagine how life will be without the problem. Most students, teachers, and parents cope better with hope and encouragement. That is why the words *will be, someday soon when, when things get better* presuppose that change is imminent. Saying *if it gets better or if things change* does not have the same effect. Students who are stuck in a problem need new thoughts to help them see their goal.

The following sequence of questions is an example of externalizing a problem of *anger*: Suppose a student complained that he was just too angry to do his schoolwork that afternoon. A teacher might get the class started on an assignment and speak to the student outside of the classroom, proposing the following types of questions to be helpful:

"Tell me about the anger that is bothering you. When do you notice 'it' being around the most?"

"When does the anger not bother you so much? How do you make that happen?"

"What are you doing differently to be free of anger during those times?"

"Who will notice when the anger is no longer bothering you so often?"

"What needs to happen with the anger so that you can do your work today in school?"

"Based on what you've just told me, what do you think you might try to make the anger less of a problem for you just for today?"

Elementary school children love the idea of externalizing problems. In my therapy office are lots of stuffed animals. Many are sweet-looking animals such as cats, dogs, a seal, a chicken, an elephant, and many teddy bears. I also have some not-so-sweet-looking animals such as a large tiger, a huge German Shepherd dog, a pink dinosaur, a yellow monster, and the Cheshire cat. When I start talking to children, I ask them to pick out an animal that looks how the problem feels sometimes. They typically choose one of the not-so-sweet-looking animals. Then, holding on tight to the stuffed toy, we discuss the following:

"What does the problem make you do when it is around?"

"Who notices that the problem is bigger than you sometimes?"

Then, after we talk about how tough the problem makes days at school or nights at home, I ask the child where he or she would like to put the problem so that we can talk for a few minutes without it. One five-year-old once opened my office door and walked her problem down the hall and placed it in a corner. When she ran back into my office, I asked her to choose another animal, one that seemed nicer and happier. She then chose from the sweet-looking assortment and we continued to talk.

"What happens to you when the problem is not around and, instead, you have a happier feeling, like right now?"

"Let's pretend that the animal is magical and you could take it with you today [and sometimes they do!]. You go home and go to sleep and tomorrow when you wake up, the animal helps you to keep away the problem. What will happen tomorrow that will be so much better?"

"Tell me who will notice when the happier animal is around instead of the problem?"

For school-related problems, the conversation can turn into the list found on the next page.

Language such as this helps students of all ages to visualize problems as external and, thereby, controllable. These questions place the child in the expert role. The teacher can simply ask questions that help students to separate themselves from the problem. Notice also that the questions request that the child refrain from the problem for very short amounts of time. This is very important since a child's attention span is quite short. For a kindergarten child or first-grade child, an afternoon is long enough to experiment. Second-, third-, and fourth-grade students can experiment for a day. Fifth-through eighth-grade students can experiment for two to three days. Adolescents should never be asked to try and gain control for longer than a week. The focus is on success—and the time frame must be conducive to success happening. When students are asked to do something for a short amount of time, the likelihood of success is better.

What my problem makes me do	How I win over the problem
It makes me get up when I am in a group.	I go sit by myself.
It makes me talk to Susie.	I turn the other way when she talks to me during reading.
It made me hit Jeremy on the playground.	I played in a different place.
It makes me rude to Ms Thomas when I think she doesn't like me.	I think she might have a bad day sometimes and I smile at her.
It makes me cry when I think about my grandmother. I miss her.	I talk to Mr James, the School Counsellor, and he helps me to remember her in a happy way.
It makes me frustrated because I can't pass Honors English like I did last year.	Change to a regular English class so I don't feel so stressed. I changed to a basic science class last year and it helped.

Additional ways to encourage students to defeat their problems

Another nice way of reminding a student of new behaviors that keep the problem away is to offer him or her a certificate. (A reproducible certificate is included at the end of Chapter Two.) David Epston and Michael White, therapists and authors of *Narrative Means to Therapeutic Ends* (1990), routinely give certificates to people. The certificate can be a surprise or a promise—whatever is appropriate for the student or parent. An example is shown on the next page

The certificate might include the "problem" description, the exceptions that helped solve the problem and the signature of the educator. This *rite of passage* can be presented during a teacher–student conference, before class, after class, or at a parent conference. Getting a surprise certificate describing what a student has done well is usually a real morale booster. Schools often give out certificates for such nonacademic work as a "best smile" and "the neatest work", all of which are keen observations of student success. Why not give out a certificate that enables a student to see him- or herself as successful over a problem? Everyone will win.

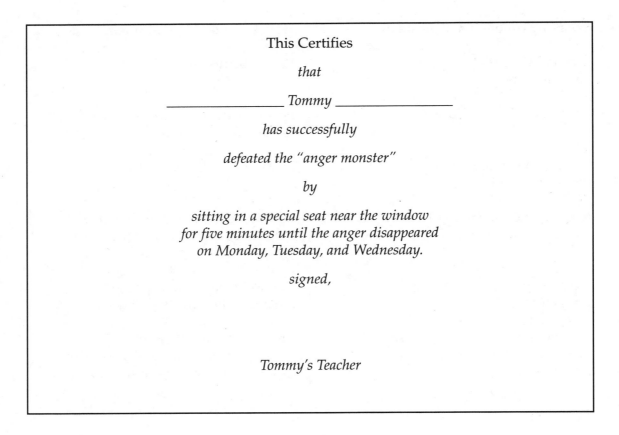

This Certifies

that

_____ *Tommy* _____

has successfully

defeated the "anger monster"

by

sitting in a special seat near the window
for five minutes until the anger disappeared
on Monday, Tuesday, and Wednesday.

signed,

Tommy's Teacher

Scaling problems down to size

Scaling questions are therapeutic tools used to *measure* the effects of a problem on a person's life (de Shazer, 1988). For example, a student, teacher, or parent can rate, on a scale of 1–10, the following:

problem is in control   student is in control

    1   2   3   4   5   6   7   8   9   10

"At 1, the problem is in total control of your school life. At 10, you are in complete control of the problem at school. Where are you?"

The student is asked to tell where he or she is as the conversation begins. Scaling questions assist school clients in defining their goals *specifically*, thereby making it easier to achieve. When school clients become "stuck" and have difficulty identifying exceptions to their concern or imagining a time when things are better, the scaling questions offer *small steps* to take to slowly progress away from the problem's influence. Scaling questions are very useful in talking to adolescents. Many secondary students have ideas as to what might help them to succeed, yet they cannot verbalize what those ideas are. By presenting a scale that helps them to designate where they are, they can begin verbalizing what a slight improvement might look like. For example:

Teacher: Kim, on a scale of 1–10 with '1' meaning you don't understand the algebra assignment from yesterday at all and '10' meaning you understand it so well you would make a '100', where are you?

Kim: About a '5', halfway, I guess.

Teacher: What can we do to get you to a '6'?

Kim: Help me to understand this exercise on page 68—that's where I get lost. Then I can do the assignment and not have this incomplete grade.

or,

Teacher: Larry, if I gave you a scale of 1–10, where '1' meant that you were not getting anything out of this class, and a '10' meant that you were getting everything you needed and were passing with an 'A,' where would you say you are right now?

Larry: I think I am at a '6'. I know that I need to do my assignments and turn them in. I just keep forgetting to turn them in when I do them.

Teacher: You know, I've noticed that when you do turn them in, you do okay. What can I do to help you remember to turn them in for a few days until you get in the habit?

Scaling questions are not intimidating; rather, they offer students the chance to choose their own strategy. The questions also give the teacher an opportunity to argue *constructively* that he or she sees the student at a higher point. The teacher who uses the idea of a scale will also find it helpful to suggest that the student move up one point at a time. Often the challenge to prove the teacher wrong can be instrumental in motivating a student to achieve more and to score higher. In the case that a student falls slightly backward, the teacher can then say quite productively:

"You know, you were at a '7' on Friday in this class and it seems like you've moved slightly backward this week. What do you suggest doing to get back up to a '7' again since you have been there so recently?"

Putting exceptions to work in the solution-focused classroom

Chapter Two has suggested consistently that watching for student exceptions to problems is the strategy for identifying solutions. It has also focused intensely on the teacher–student relationship and cultivating that relationship as another strategy to student success and self confidence. While the search for exceptions in students can make the difference between students seeing their abilities or not, this strategy also applies to teachers and *their* discovery of relationship skills!

Whenever you find yourself stuck in a tug-of-war with a student, parent, or even a colleague, chances are you are being problem focused and are not cooperating with the needs of the other person. One way to step out of the struggle and onto a better path is to look at your own personal strengths in dealing with people in your personal life. In Chapter Three you will be presented with an inventory to assist you in identifying the way you deal with stress and problem solving. Today's students need an individual approach that appeals to their individual needs. Many of us have good friends, children, and significant others whom we cherish in our lives, yet who still frustrate us at times; we are careful, however, of what we say and what we do around them. Because of our emotional bond with them, we are sometimes able to see past the frustrating actions as unsuccessful attempts to get our attention, help them to solve problems, or communicate their concern to us. When we take on this new insight, our responses discourage arguments and the frustrating person sees that—while his or her strategy does not accomplish anything—we are still there for that person.

Concluding comments

The way we describe our world says much about how we live and work. As educators, if we can assist students, teachers, and parents in perceiving their world differently and encourage hope and success, we give them a way of rewriting their lives into more successful stories. Like any other successful story, this task takes editing and changing the way the characters move through their system. By redirecting the characters towards scenes in which they appear competent and skillful, the teacher has an opportunity to influence the conclusion of such a story in the most profound way.

Chapter Two Practice Exercise
Learning to Build Solutions

This exercise, which deals with a school issue, will help you to begin thinking in a more solution-focused manner. Think of the most challenging situation you might have at school at this moment. After you complete the exercise, think about a current personal dilemma you might have and use the same questions to help you find new ideas of dealing with that as well.

The Problem Focus

Recall, for a moment, a problem that may be challenging you at school this year. Write it here:

_____

_____

What has to change for things to be better?

_____

_____

What strategies have you tried to reach your goal? List those strategies here.

1. _____

2. _____

3. _____

4. _____

5. _____

Which of these strategies worked best? Place a check by those.

Which of the strategies did not work? Put a line through those.

The Solution Focus

Write below how things will be—in a literal sense—when the problem bothering you at school is no longer so much a problem. What will **you** be doing (not anyone else) when that happens?

_____

_____

_____

Learning to Build Solutions *(continued)*

If the problem involves someone else needing to change, what would that person need to do to free you from the problem? What would that enable you to do?

_____

_____

_____

Think back to other times when you were able to accomplish a little of your goal in that situation or in similar situations. (Consider strengths in your personal life, in other relationships, or skills in other job areas.) What did you do then that seemed to work? (If the problem is a person, think of ways/times when you did something different in spite of a person who was not willing to change.)

_____

_____

_____

Think also of times when the problem was not so influential in your day. Write what your behaviors or thinking was during those times:

_____

_____

_____

Think of what your colleagues, friends, or family members would say you do to accomplish similar goals such as this one, even if only slightly.

1. _____

2. _____

3. _____

What could you begin to do on a small scale, using the strategies that you just listed?

_____

_____

_____

Certificate of Success

This certifies that

_____

has successfully

_____

_____

This success was achieved by the following:

_____

Signed, this _____ day of _____, _____

Chapter Three
Working with the Challenging Student

"Never let school interfere with your education."

—Mark Twain

An experienced elementary teacher, Peggy Ellrod of Arlington, Texas, contributed the following dilemma:

"Help me learn to deal with students and adults who have little respect for themselves and others. This week I had a child sleep through class. Later I discovered that he had been beaten the night before. The beating was not severe enough to be reported, we were told. How, oh, how could I survive under those circumstances? All I know to do is to just smile, hug and love him!"

Ms. Ellrod's actions speak louder than any words could ever say! How fortunate for the student to have someone like her in his life. How fortunate for her that *she* had learned to ask before reacting. She altered the child's outlook at the world for at least a moment with her kindness in the midst of his misery. He will probably never forget her understanding and touch on a day when going home promised to be a terrifying experience.

Of all the chapters in this book, Chapter Three was the most difficult to write because the needs that are addressed in it captured my heart and challenged my ideas. In order to write a helpful chapter, I asked teachers who taught at all levels to fill out a questionnaire and describe to me what they needed from a book like this. Their responses appear throughout the chapter and will serve as a guide for discussion. In addition to teacher responses, I interviewed students and compared the teacher concerns with student observations of those teachers. The student responses proved to be quite valuable and paved the way for more insight into how to reach and teach them. Due to the nature of the questionnaires and student responses, Chapter Three may contain statements that may challenge the thinking of those who feel that children must be ready to learn and respectful before they can be taught. There will be suggestions made for teachers who feel frustrated and defensive that at first may seem to be unfair and uncomfortable.

The chapter carries a theme: to look beyond the behavior or deficits of a child and turn within oneself for answers to reach and teach the most challenging students. This chapter is not about teachers and students as we have come to know them; it is about viewing ourselves as trainers and our students as apprentices in a world that sometimes influences them to get off track morally, behaviorally, and emotionally. To get them back on track we must adhere to our own personal morals, different behaviors, and emotional support—and step outside of their system to do so. We can't get caught up in the behavior that we are trying to dissolve in the classroom. Get ready. Chapter Three was *written* by you and your students for both of you.

Retraining the challenging student

How can a child learn when she is told the night before by her mother: "I hate you and your father so I am leaving." How can an adolescent study for her biology exam when her stepfather touches her inappropriately? How can a junior high boy think of the preventive drug program he is learning about at school when his mother is smoking marijuana in the next room? They can't. Instead, they come to school and they don't think, learn, or communicate their needs to us in ways that we can understand. They communicate all right, in an inexperienced, inappropriate manner that they have learned from their world. A colleague, Ina Crowe, a school counselor and special education teacher, offers the following wisdom and encourages us to look at such students differently:

"When someone says that a student is lazy or that she doesn't care, I see it as a red flag that I must pay attention to the student. Most of the time when I talk to the student, I learn that she is depressed or that her home life is in shambles. Then I go to work to be supportive and work for her until she sees that I will be a person who will never give up on her. And I don't give up. Pretty soon she is working for me. It works."

The solution-focused teacher knows that a child or adolescent who raises red flags through misbehavior, miscommunication, or poor academic performance often needs the opposite of what he or she is instigating or communicating. The student needs an unexpected response from his teacher so that he sees that his misbehavior does not work for him. This means the teacher must do *something different*. It does not mean that the teacher must give in, cater to, or be inconsistent with the student. Nor does it mean that the teacher will *lose* control of the class because she does something unpredictable with Joey. Chances are, the class knows how difficult Joey is. They are intuitive as to what the teacher is doing and appreciate the teacher calming Joey no matter what it takes. The teacher uses her personal skills to make a difference for Joey. On the survey for problem solving, jot down some of your own personal skills in dealing with stress and conflict. Chances are you are more talented than you realize and your students will benefit when you begin to use those talents.

A Personal Survey for Problem-Solving

Problem: Conflict

Solutions for handling conflict in the classroom

When faced with a difference of opinion or a behavior that is dissimilar to yours, do you typically confront persons who are important to you or do you work out the differences together?

_____

_____

_____

Which method seems to have the best result?

_____

_____

What are you thinking about that helps you to respond in that way?

_____

_____

What would your friends or significant others say that you do in that situation that makes such a difference for them that they *listen or respond to you positively?*

_____

_____

Problem: How do I help someone who is hurt, stressed, or frustrated?

Solutions for helping students who are hurt, stressed, or frustrated

What do you do when significant others are hurt, feeling stressed, and frustrated, and they take it out on you?

_____

_____

What do you think about the person before you talk or act?

_____

_____

What do you say to someone who is stressed and frustrated, yet whom you know has been successful in taking charge of a similar situation before?

_____

_____

What do you do or how do you console someone important to you when he or she is sad?

_____

_____

A Personal Survey for Problem-Solving *(continued)*

Problem: Dealing with people who lack basic information

How do you relay information to close friends who are ignorant of basic information in a respectful manner so they want to listen and are not offended?

What do you think about so that you come across respectfully and not condescending?

How do you stay calm and patient?

Solutions for respectfully dealing with students who lack basic information

_____

_____

_____

_____

_____

_____

Problem: You're stressed!

Stress can often take over our lives and intrude. How do you deal with stress effectively so that it does not intrude on your ability to come across sincere to those persons important to you?

What do you think about so that you do not take out your concerns on others?

What do you say to significant people in your life so that they know they are not the problem?

How do you ask for help during stressful times, so that people comply with you in a kind manner?

Solutions for handling stress in the classroom

_____

_____

_____

_____

_____

_____

_____

_____

(This exercise was adapted from the ideas of Furman and Ahola in *Reteaming, Succeeding Together*, 1997)

Personal skills that work in the classroom

The skills that a teacher possesses in personal relationships can provide him or her with an outline of strategies for the classroom. Not only do the skills help the teacher deal with students differently, they are comfortable, natural interpersonal skills that will probably be consistent over time. The following cases show how teachers approached students with a solution-focused strategy, *reinforced by their personal skills* that worked for them in other situations.

Cindy

The student
Cindy, age 10, failed her spelling test *again* with a 65 because she did not study or listen to the review given by Ms. Kennedy. Upset, she wadded up her paper and threw it on the floor. It is January and Cindy made 80s and 90s during the fall.

The teacher
Ms. Kennedy is a personable person who has many close friends. She considers herself to be a kind person who tends to listen to close friends and relatives rather than to confront them. Because of this trait she is often surrounded by colleagues in the teacher's lounge who receive lots of encouragement from her.

The teacher's strategy
"Cindy, you know, I was looking at my grade book and realized something incredible. Look at it with me. See all of those 80s and 90s last semester? They were yours. What do you think you did differently last fall to make grades like these?

"I also remember that when you listened to the review and studied with a friend in class, you did well. I'm going to let you choose a study partner today. You can both sit in the hallway or go to the library to go over the words on Thursday. You know how to score a high grade. I'm going to be so excited for you when you do it next week."

The result
Cindy's mother called the teacher and asked what she was doing differently at school because her daughter was coming home so happy. Cindy began passing her spelling tests and Ms. Kennedy continued to give her all the credit when she did so well, always asking *Cindy* for her secret.

Roger

The student

Roger, age 15, had never taken an honors class. Content to go to school and make average grades, he enjoyed other activities and was not interested in excelling past what was expected of him. As he entered high school, his counselor placed him in an honors English class *just to see how he would do*, since his achievement tests indicated that he was well above average in language. One day in  the honors class, he realized that he had not completed his homework definitions. He hurriedly made up some definitions and was almost finished when his teacher, Ms. Cox, approached him and *caught him red-handed, filling in the blanks!*

The teacher

Ms. Cox was the Student Council Sponsor. Her love of teaching was so obvious to her students that she rarely had a free moment by herself at school. Surrounded by students wherever she went in the high school, she was always seen joking with kids, smiling and teasing them with her sweet sense of humor and kindness. She tended to associate with colleagues like herself who had a kind demeanor towards their students. She was a determined teacher, too, who saw through students' tough exteriors and always responded in a way that melted their resistance and defensiveness. She knew no enemies, it seemed, and her students rarely, if ever, defied her.

The teacher's strategy

"Roger, these are unique and clever answers. Did you make them up yourself?" [Student nods and smiles shyly.] You do realize that your grade won't be quite so high as it could be since you made them up, but wow, you know, I like these. I especially like this one! Why don't you look up the rest of the words and turn those in at the end of class."

The result

In all of Roger's school years, he had never encountered a teacher like Ms. Cox. When he wrote an essay, she would look past the grammar and praise his insight and ability to express himself which was well above what his other classmates did. His competency was her focus, and he blossomed under her wings into a student who wanted to excel. The next year he took all honors courses. This year, as I write this book, that student, my son, Roger, has applied to some of the top universities in the country, with a goal of being a writer, and he's graduating in the top percentage of his senior class. What did Ms. Cox do to motivate a student who typically settled for average grades? In her words, "Sometimes you have to look past things so as to not burn out the candle in a student. You have to see the whole student. Roger had insight and who was I to be inflexible? I had to find a way to challenge and expect things from him without discouraging who he was."

Armando

The student
Armando, age 20, was a junior in a high school where drugs and violence were so common that police officers roamed the hallways and teachers were desperate to get order so that they could teach a lesson. He often slept when he came into English class, so as he approached the spring semester, he was anxious to *break in the new teacher*. He was attending school because he truly wanted to graduate, yet school was boring to him and his grades were failing.

The teacher
A first-year teacher, Ms. Angell was told there were several students who slept through class and she would be wise to let them sleep, since they were less disruptive that way. She was amazed at how the other teachers yelled at the students in the hallways. Walking through the hallways, she often felt as if she were taking her life in her own hands. In her personal life, she had learned always to persevere. She had been a law student who realized soon after beginning her second year of law school, that the rigidity and nonemotional approach to law did not fit her views about people. She switched gears, applied for teacher education certification, and realized that she had finally found her niche.

The strategy
Ms. Angell looked at Armando as someone significant. He was 20, sitting in a room with 16-year-olds. How bored he must be, she thought. She had been told that he was only at school to sell drugs. She put that rumor aside. Instead of allowing him to sleep, she decided to walk or stand by him often, gently touching his arm or shoulder, prompting him to "listen to something interesting." After class, she would often ask him to stay and talk about how *he* thought the class was going. She listened to his suggestions. She kept talking to him and praising him for any work that he did.

The result
Armando began to participate in English class. If he looked sleepy, Ms. Angell would prod him for answers and would not let him leave the classroom until he turned in his work. He began to pass English. When I observed her teaching recently, all eyes were on her and her charm and verbal prompting kept them on track. Armando was paying attention too.

Developing solutions to classroom dilemmas

I talked with many teachers while writing this book and asked them what they needed most in their classrooms. The following is a result of their requests.

Classroom dilemma #1: The student is disrespectful, disruptive, and unmotivated

"Help me to deal with students who are not motivated, are disrespectful, and have no respect for authority. For them, school is not a priority. Their parents are often irritated that we do not handle the problem at school."

"I need ways to reach students with little or no self motivation."

"One of my students assaulted a vice principal and 911 was called. Help. I'm afraid."

"My greatest challenge was a student I had last year. His behavior was unbelievable! I had no parental support and little administrative help. This year the same student threatened the principal with a knife. We are getting more and more of these students."

Classroom solution #1

Disrespectful students *expect* to be confronted, which leads to more confrontation. Do the unexpected ... stay calm and do something different so the student's disrespectful attitude *doesn't work*. Keep the dangerous student safe from others and build a better relationship immediately if the student returns to the classroom.

The following case study is an example of a teacher/trainer who used solution-focused thinking to change the disruptive, disrespectful behavior of a young man whom others had given up on (Metcalf, 1997, pp. 142–144). As you read the case, notice how different the solution-focused approach is compared with what happens in classrooms with a problem approach.

Getting off on the right foot: A case study

Mr. Cross, a drama teacher, warmly welcomed Jose, a junior high student returning from alternative school, into his classroom. As Jose began to disrupt the class, Mr. Cross tried several ways to redirect him, yet Jose did not respond. Ultimately, Mr. Cross sent Jose to the office for a discipline pass. Jose returned to the class ten minutes later with the discipline pass chewed up in his mouth. He walked over to Mr. Cross, who was standing in front of the class, and spit it on his shoe. Thinking hurriedly, with 30 other students silently waiting for chaos to emerge, Mr. Cross told Jose:

"Jose, you know, I can't read this very well. Would you mind smoothing it out for me, or going to get another pass?"

Surprised, Jose walked out of the class to get another pass. No one had responded to his antics like this before! He returned ten minutes later with a new pass, laid it on Mr. Cross's desk, and Mr. Cross thanked him. Throughout the class period, whenever Jose doodled on a worksheet or paper, Mr. Cross would compliment him on his artwork. The next day, early in the morning before school, Jose walked into Mr. Cross's classroom and said:

"Mr. Cross, man, I'm sorry about yesterday."

Jose stayed in school for most of the semester. He and Mr. Cross would do "high five's" in the hallway, surprising many of Jose's teachers. Jose's attitude had changed. He was now participating in set design for a play, at the encouragement of Mr. Cross. He had changed his attitude in most of his classes. One day in drama class, a fight broke out in the back of the room. Jose got up to participate, stopped, then turned around and put his head on his desk. Mr. Cross noticed. He went to his computer that afternoon after class and wrote Jose a note.

Dear Jose,

I was quite impressed with you yesterday. You got up to fight but then you sat down. It took a lot of courage to do that! You have done an outstanding job this semester in my class. You are a great contribution to our decoration committee. I am proud to have you as my student!

Sincerely,

Mr. Cross

When Mr. Cross gave Jose the letter on official school stationery, Jose read it and said:

"Man, I can take this note home and I won't get hit for this one."

The end of resistance

Mr. Cross knew that resistance disappears when teachers change directions with a student. A solution-focused teacher always does something different or unpredictable when she senses that a confrontation might occur between her and a student by using a solution-focused way of thinking. The solution-focused teacher does not focus on making the student recognize who is in charge; rather, the teacher focuses on letting the student know that she is committed to resolving the problem. She does this by not getting defensive and offensive; instead, she keeps herself calm and collected, sending a message to her student that his actions will not get him anywhere. The following words are good to remember when faced with a behaviorally challenging student:

"Don't respond to this behavior defensively with a problem-focus or it will multiply. As I talk to this student, I will be nonaccusatory, nonthreatening and I will ask what it will take for us to be able to work together, offering my part first. I will model for the student a different way for him to respond. I will also remember that he may not respond well at first, but I must persevere."

The R.E.S.T. will follow

As the interaction progresses, the teacher can keep the R.E.S.T. acronym in mind to help him or her think more toward solutions:

R   **Redescribe the behavior of the student.** Changing your thinking about a student will give you a chance to be more creative with your strategies.

E   **Examine the exceptions to the student's actions.** Look for times when you are more successful in gaining student attention or when the student is slightly more successful.

S   **Strategize and plan a new reaction to the student.** Think of your past strategies, identify which ones did not work, and don't repeat them. Instead, repeat strategies that worked occasionally and examine how the strategies made a difference. Repeat those.

T   **Teach your student that you respect him or her no matter what!** Through your actions and words, send a message to your student that you are committed to keeping the relationship kind and communicative.

Taking action in this way does not mean that a classroom management program needs to be abandoned for the sake of one student, but it does mean that the classroom management must be flexible enough to accommodate the need of such a student so that the other students can experience a better environment. Such attention can consist of a note such as the one written by Mr. Cross, or an unexpected compliment about an assignment or comment made in class. It can be as simple as standing by a student's desk and smiling or telling him personally how much his attention was appreciated during the video. Mr. Cross could have treated Jose as the other teachers did when he misbehaved, but that would have perpetuated Jose's typically unruly behavior and kept Jose in the same context of being a troublemaker, a reputation that he had amply fulfilled in the past. By doing the unexpected, Mr. Cross increased the odds that Jose would do something different. His new perception of Jose changed Jose's perception of himself, creating new behaviors as a result. Both teacher and student flourished in this new environment.

Teachers expect students to respect authority, and for good reason! However, how can they look at the world positively when their parents are in jail, or when the authority who is supposed to love them, beats them and calls them names. They have learned to disrespect others and the only way back on track to living a respectful life is by experiencing repeatedly an environment in which disrespect is *not* allowed ... by anyone. Teachers must supply the training for those students in their classroom through offering validation, acceptance, and bonding that parents did not supply so that learning can happen! Without these efforts teachers will continue to be yelled at, threatened, and ignored. These behaviors are adult behaviors that have been learned. We must think of ourselves as trainers who have the trainees six hours a day. As with all new training, we must gain their attention and, while we have it, we must make a difference.

One way to gain the attention of the student is through conducting a sort of experiment on the student's behavior, redescribed as a "habit". *The Formula First Session Task*, as suggested by Steve de Shazer, is a helpful way to assist students in identifying exceptions to their academic life, behavior, and emotional stability. The Task lowers resistance and places responsibility on the child or adolescent to watch his or her own behavior, thereby changing the process of the behavior. The task can be described as an *experiment*, and is given simply as a means for the student to learn how to notice when school works. If a school client is unable to name a specific problem, he or she can simply watch for *any* time over the next few days when he or she enjoys or feels more successful at school. As the school client attends to the task of noticing when school works, he or she often will act differently in class. This same assignment is effective for teachers and administrators who can't find time to attend to their own issues with teaching. Asking educators to notice when their job is less stressful, more effective, or consistent encourages them to begin to see their job differently. For most people, a new outlook can enhance a stressful situation. (A reproducible page for the *Formula First Session Task* is included at the end of Chapter Three.)

Experimenting with the Formula First Session Task

Formula First Session Task

(adapted from De Shazer, 1985)

For the next few days, I'm going to be watching for the times when you move away from the behaviors that bother you in my class. I'm going to be watching for times when you are paying attention, doing your work, or behaving differently. I'm going to write those times down and you can take the note home to your parents if you like.

I'd also like for you to notice times in the classroom when you don't find yourself getting off track. Would you notice what I do that seems to help? I am very interested in your ideas.

I have to caution you that it's sometimes hard to break a habit, so we will both have to really try and look for what works instead of what doesn't.

Classroom dilemma #2: The student is smart but is not serious about learning

"Help me deal with the pressure of having to find a way to pass the kids who do no homework or class work."

"Teachers cannot just teach! We have so much paper work, charts, achievement test preparations . . . do this, do that. . . . We wish that we could just come in, do our job, and plan for our children."

"I need real solutions for the 2% of students who rarely do their work, talk constantly and disrupt the class."

Classroom solution #2
Watch for the student's interest and capitalize on them with compliments, not praise, by asking: "How were you able to draw such an interesting picture . . . write such a short, but clever essay . . . manage to pay attention for a few minutes?" Send a message to the student that you will not give up until he or she succeeds. Allow the exceptions to the problem to guide you towards better interventions.

Going above and beyond: A case study

When I met her three years ago, I was immediately impressed by her energy. Walking into her portable classroom that evening, I was greeted with an excited handshake by one of son's new high school teachers. "I am so honored to have your son in my class this year. It is a true pleasure!" she said. Surprised, I half wondered if she were real. As our conversation continued and she described the course that she would teach my son over the next nine months, I began to wish that I was back in high school so that I could sit in on her class myself. As a teacher relatively new in her field, I wondered if her excitement would last. As I watched her over the year and listened to my son describe his assignments, his thoughts, and the enjoyment of being in her class, I realized that her excitement did last. In fact, it seemed to multiply, extending beyond the classroom with hallway conversations and motivational advice as he finished other high school courses. My son and I experienced something that we would both remember. He was taught by Larissa Cox, a classroom teacher who loved what she did and transferred her love of learning to her students. It was after being a student in her class that my son began to take school more seriously and see himself differently.

Many of us can recall the teacher who challenged us and made us think differently. That teacher motivated us to become what we only wished we could be. Who was yours? What did he or she do that made such a difference? Did he inspire you to become a teacher or, did she believe in you enough so that you perceived your future positively, setting you free to persevere? My memorable teacher came late in my school career. Dr. Frank Thomas was a teacher in my graduate school program at Texas Woman's University whose excitement for solution-focused thinking and dramatic respect for people's competencies turned my head in a completely different direction after attending the first of his many classes. He continued to be my mentor and, later, my major professor, encouraging and instigating my first published article. What are the ingredients possessed by those mighty educators who send us messages of excitement, motivation, and intrigue in their subjects? The answers seem to lie within the personal relationships that they developed between themselves and their students which opened the door of discovery to the student, making learning meaningful and lasting. Those special teachers did something that our other teachers forgot to do. They believed in us enough to convince us that we could do whatever we wanted, sometimes without their ever saying it!

When I approached Larissa Cox and asked her to contribute a story for this book, she shared with me the following story of "Joe". As you read about Joe's evolution in her classroom, consider how a problem-focused teacher might have approached a student similar to Joe. Then, notice how effective and *simple* the solution-focused approach was that Ms. Cox used, focusing on Joe's strengths and determined to do something different to reach him. Read how the relationship that she chose to have with him served as an alternative pathway so that Joe's direction collided with Ms. Cox's!

Don't be a "Miss Caroline"*: A case study

In Harper Lee's classic novel *To Kill a Mockingbird*, Scout finds herself in trouble on her very first day of school. Her crime? She already knows how to read. "Now you tell your father not to teach you any more," commands Miss Caroline, her teacher (Lee 17). Aside from her problems with the teacher–parent relationship, Miss Caroline has indicated that the child's prior knowledge is a bad thing. Scout reflects:

> I mumbled that I was sorry and retired meditating upon my crime. I never deliberately learned to read ... I could not remember when the lines above Atticus's moving finger separated into words ... (I read) anything Atticus happened to be reading when I crawled into his lap every night. Until I feared I would lose it, I never loved to read. One does not love breathing.

Breathing? Yes, she compares reading to the unconscious, natural act of inhaling and exhaling. And that is what reading—and learning in general—is to an innocent child from the moment of his or her first breath. But then something happens; a "Miss Caroline" comes along. In the novel, Miss Caroline also encounters a student with no lunch money and a student with "cooties". She handles these students poorly as well. Neither her youth nor her inexperience are her faults; it is her inability to meet the child right where she is.

I currently have a student in my third period class who is clever. He is also lazy. It is a comical combination. He likes to "complete" assignments and respond to written questions with trenchant and ingenious expositions that absolutely do not meet the requirements of the task. I am assuming that in some classrooms, he gets a tickle from writing these outlandish creations and even more of a laugh from the fact that many teachers just skim or "check" the assignment for completion; thereby, he receives a grade and they are never the wiser. I'm positive that he also gets a thrill from those teachers who respond with anger to his ridiculous antics.

But I have thrown him; I actually like what he writes. He often provides elaborate explanations of why it is I who have asked a poor question. Other times he attempts to prove the irreverence of the topic at hand. He also has an extensive repertoire of logical reasons why he does not know the answer. His responses are always lengthy, humorous, and well thought out. I read every word and comment on it all. I commend his creativity. I point out and praise his logical and critical thinking. I also point out the moments that he actually does breech the subject at hand. Finally, I grade him fairly and accurately. While he may sometimes write a great response to a question, if it does not address the question I may give him half credit for trying. He likes that I read his work

---

*"Don't Be a 'Miss Caroline' " has been contributed by Larissa Cox, who is currently a teacher at The Woodlands High School in Spring, Texas. In 1997, she left Mansfield High School where her students dedicated their yearbook to her, citing her as a teacher who always "went above and beyond what was expected".

and respond to it; he is also disappointed in his grade. For whatever reason, he wants to please me. Slowly and gradually, he is starting to use that wit and creativity on task and on topic. It is amazing. I am so proud of him. One wrong move on my part, however, and I might have lost him forever.

No matter what a student comes to us with, it is our job as teachers to assess the child—then take him or her forward. Yes, the pressure is high. The responsibilities of a teacher are immeasurable, critical, and often irreversible. Granted, the ultimate responsibility lies with the student; however, deep down, at some point, all children do want to learn and it is our job to try to make that happen and provide an environment where it can. For example, in my classroom, if something is not working, nine times out of ten it is my fault. If Lindsay is reading a magazine instead of reading *Julius Caesar*, it is because I have not engaged her in the task. I have found that making my expectations painfully clear helps students tremendously. If all I want them to have on their desk is their liter-ature book, a piece of paper, and a pen, they do not know this and will not do this unless I specifically ask them to do so. In addition, it is pointless to proceed until everyone is ready. My 15- and 16-year-old sophomores love that whoever has said items on their desk first is going to be verbally recognized by me. I simply say, "Look at Kelli! She's a model student! If you are wondering what you should be doing right now, look at Kelli!" It's fantastic when the most distracted, disinterested student in the class is yelling out, "Hey, Mrs. Cox, look at me! I'm a model student, too!" I call it positive peer pressure, and it works.

Reading and learning should be like breathing! Unfortunately somewhere along the way things change, and learning becomes more like ancient Chinese torture. If only Miss Caroline, upon discovering Scout's early reading capabilities, had said:

"Why Scout, I'm so impressed with your abilities! I will really need your leadership in class this year! And guess what else, I'm going to help you read even more and even better! Won't your father be pleased the next time you read together!"

Imagine how differently Scout would have perceived herself after such a compliment! Students come to us in all conditions: excited, sad, hurt, hyper, clever, brilliant, lazy—and yes—even with cooties. One accusation, one negative reaction, one careless moment can cause that student to lose heart, to lose face, and to lose faith. Teaching is hard. It is the teacher's job to meet the needs of each individual student and then take the group forward as a whole, keeping in mind that many students have had a "Miss Caroline" or two in their past and don't want to go anywhere. I am saddened each year by the number of students who are surprised that I actually care about them and their learning and that I like them, cooties and all. We as teachers must be willing to modify and adjust, revamp and rework both our plans and our ideas. We must be open to the very essence of what makes each child unique. In doing so, we reveal the true potential in not only the child, but in ourselves.

Just for today, reach one student

Today's teacher is overwhelmed with regulations, paperwork, and students! To even suggest that he or she consider the emotional and individual academic needs of each

student seems outlandish but important. It may be more helpful to think of that situation differently. Ms. Cox thought out her strategy for motivating Joe, one student, in contrast to what his other teachers had not done in the past. By watching her response to Joe, Ms. Cox changed Joe's responses and motivated him in the process. This kept the atmosphere in her classroom appropriate. When one challenging student such as Joe changes in a classroom of 30 students, the atmosphere of the entire class changes dramatically, making it well worth the teacher's effort. The other students begin to notice how the student is being approached and become the teacher's ally since they see her trying hard to reach their peer. Imagine how different your classroom would be tomorrow if the one or two students who typically acted out, behaved and cooperated. Perhaps, instead of thinking:

"I don't have time to spend on him when there are twenty-nine others ..."

... you might think instead:

"How can I react differently to this student just for today so that the entire class runs differently?"

This may result in your writing down what you have tried with the student and erasing those strategies that were ineffective. It means thinking that "I haven't found the way to gain his attention and respect yet. I need to keep on watching for what makes him interested" instead of waiting for the student to change. Devising such a strategy for two or three students out of 30 seems more achievable—and when the strategy is collaborated with colleagues or a team, it gives the teacher hope. Besides, students know when a teacher goes above and beyond for them to figure out and design a new way of learning and relating. Those are the teachers the *students* remember. Their efforts to know them and share information convey a silent message that "I must be worth my teacher's time!"

The worksheet "Brainstorming New Motivational Strategies" can serve as a way to brainstorm new possibilities for the most challenging of students. Whether it is the 6-year-old who talks out and always seems to forget to raise his hand, the 10-year-old who refuses to sit quietly, or the 14-year-old whose off-color comments are driving you crazy, thinking of something new to do or say *will* result in a different outcome and change your relationship.

Classroom dilemma #3: The student has no home support

"I have to find a way to incorporate moral values with today's lifestyles."

"Help me to help the kids overcome a negative home environment. Their parents are noncaring, nonnurturing, and uninvolved."

"Where do I start? A child yelled—in my class and I had her call her mother. The mother said I was unfair and picked on her child. After all, she said, the word was a bodily function!"

Classroom solution #3

Become the student's support system away from home, regardless of whether you think you can make a difference, because you will! Put aside the belief that the home must be supportive in order for the child to learn. When parents do not follow through, model for the child that you are an adult he or she can believe in. Help the child to discover ways to cope by using solution-focused questions that instill hope and prove to the child that he or she can manage.

Years ago it made sense to control and correct behaviors of students who were not living up to the school's expectations. Those were days in which schools had more respect from their communities and parental support was always available for the teacher and administrator. Today, schools are fortunate if they are able to reach parents by phone. Due to the lack of parental support, parental problems, and constant blame that parents place on the school to solve every problem, the teacher must find the way to reach her students with a different approach. The parental problems are not and should not be defined as the child's problem. The teacher must give the students what they are often not given even at home ... time, respect, and perseverance to succeed. The solution-focused teacher sees a poor home environment simply as a poor source of information for the student, not as a deterrent to the child's future. She realizes that she has the student for six hours per day and is determined to show the student a new way of relating for over 30 hours per week.

In the following case study, an elementary teacher gives a student a reason to respect himself and see himself as competent in a world where the adults were threatening and

Brainstorming New Motivational Strategies

The following solution-focused ideas and questions are helpful when a new direction is needed to reach challenging students. The questions can be worked through by the individual classroom teacher, administrator, or a team of teachers.

1. Check out what has not worked before with the student and stop doing it.

"What have I tried doing with this student that has not worked?"

_____

_____

"How can I cooperate with this student? If his actions were messages (both positive and negative), what are they saying and how can I let him know I am listening and noticing?"

_____

_____

2. Develop a personal goal for yourself to reach the student differently.

"What is my goal for this student, academically?"

_____

_____

"What can I do or say to help the student recognize that I have this goal for her?"

_____

_____

"What would the student say were signs that I was understanding her needs better?"

_____

_____

3. Check out what works with the student. Learn to cooperate so that resistant dissolves.

"When is it that I have this student's attention, even slightly?"

_____

_____

Brainstorming New Motivational Strategies *(continued)*

"When in the past did the student seem more interested in the class?"

_____

_____

"How can I respond to him so that he knows he has my attention, just for today?"

_____

_____

"What can I do to show him something interesting that I notice today, about himself?"

_____

_____

4. Observe behaviors or actions by the student that indicate interest or performance in other classes and recognize what happens in those classes as solutions.

"What did I do or say that made a difference with her today?"

_____

_____

"Where was I in the classroom, and what was I talking about or doing when these behaviors or actions happened?"

_____

_____

5. Talk to the student and let her know that you are interested in what she thinks you can do to make the class more helpful to her. Challenge her to look for exceptions.

"What do we do in here sometimes that helps you to learn better? I am interested."

_____

_____

"What do you need from me as your teacher?"

_____

_____

nonsupportive. While the teacher fought the struggle internally, she presented herself as oblivious to the student's behavior and, instead, won the student over through modeling friendliness and support.

Don't misinterpret my silence: A case study

Tim loved school. It was so much better than being at home. It was well known that his father brought friends home to drink during the week and that his mother yelled all night for them to leave. She often told the school counselor her problems and the school counselor had given her names of counselors to see privately, even though she never made an appointment. Tim was capable and sometimes shy yet he always finished his work and was eager to sit by the teacher's desk and help her with classroom chores.

Because of Tim's cheerfulness, it seemed odd for him to come to school and stiffly refuse to do work. All he wanted to do was sit still in his seat. Ms. Kaletta knew him too well and suspected that something was wrong. She asked him what the matter was and he did not reply. He just stared into her eyes and conveyed a message of "please don't ask because I'm embarrassed to tell you". Fortunately she did persist as she asked him to step out into the hallway. When she went to touch his arm, he flinched with pain. "I got beat up last night by one of my Dad's friends' kid. He was fourteen and nobody stopped him." The teacher held him for a moment and then took him down to the office. Later that day the incident was reported to the Child Abuse Hotline. Tim's family was also notified about the pain Tim experienced. While the family refused counseling, saying that they would be more alert to things happening at home, Tim's teacher and school counselor did additional interventions with Tim so that he would be ready if another incident happened again. The following dialogue is similar to the one used by Tim's teacher:

"You are a brave young man and I am impressed that you told me what happened. I wonder, has there ever been other times when you were afraid at home and you took care of yourself so that you would be safe? What did you do, exactly? How were you able to do that?"

"What about other places and times when you felt afraid—what else did you do? Was there someone you told or a place that you went to feel safe?"

These questions are noninvasive, respectful, and preventative. They focus on the child's strengths and help him to prepare for a future incident. Such preventative questions give a child a plan to follow if life becomes threatening again.

Assisting students who are emotionally volatile

Imagine being ten years old and being told by your father with anger "My girlfriend is first in my life, not you." How effective would you be at school? How much would you want to visit your father? How important do you think you would feel? When families divorce, more than parents are divided—so are the feelings of children and adolescents.

The child sees things in *logical* terms:

1. My parents are divorced. They don't like each other. Things will never be the same even though they try and tell me things are better. Things will never be better.

2. My father (or mother) says I will see him (her) every other week. That seems like a long time.

3. I want to spend time with my father (mother) by myself. When he (she) spends time with his (her) girlfriend (boyfriend), I don't feel like he (she) likes me any more. When he (she) didn't come last week, I wondered if I would ever see him (her) again. He (She) likes his (her) girlfriend (boyfriend) more than me because he (she) spends more time with her (him).

As a result, children of divorce whose parents do not fulfill their emotional needs often react at school with misbehaviors, anger, poor school performance, and sad statements. These changed behaviors cry out for validation, love, and acceptance. If the child does not receive them at home after a few calls to the parent(s), the teacher can assist the child by giving him or her what is missing:

- extra attention
- extra time on homework assignments
- extra assistance in completing class work
- listening and using solution-focused questions to build confidence
- validating ideas and performance

Whenever the child performs slightly better, the teacher can exclaim:

"Wow, you are incredible today. How were you able to complete the assignment on time? How were you able to read to yourself so quietly?"

The adolescent sees things in *emotional* terms:

1. I do not feel important to my father (mother) since he (she) left. He (She) has someone else in his (her) life who means more to him (her) than I do and I don't like her (him). I am glad he (she) and my mother (father) don't fight so much but I still feel like he (she) abandoned me. We used to be close.

2. I want my family to be whole again. I want to be like my friend's family who is still together. I feel broken, too.

3. I am angry that my father (mother) didn't come last weekend like he (she) said he (she) would. I think that I am not important to him (her) like I used to be. I feel hurt and betrayed. I'm never going to let him (her) get close to me again because it hurts so bad.

For the adolescent, offering to talk after class can be very helpful. The teacher need not inquire about details to be helpful; the teacher can refer to the situation simply as the "situation." Adolescents are very verbal and have more life experience with which to problem solve. However, their emotional needs are similar to the child's. Use solution-

focused questions to explore their ways of coping with the stressful situation so that they begin to notice that they *are* coping:

"You are in a really stressful situation. Tell me, how do you manage to even come to school?"

"How are you able to still participate in softball?"

"I wonder, since you keep on going even when things are rough, what does that say about the kind of person you are?"

These questions build confidence and competency at a time when the adolescent feels that his life is out of control. Realizing that he continues some activities and that there is an adult who realizes what he is going through and recognizes his strengths, lends acceptance at a time when the adolescent may feel his family doesn't accept him.

Classroom dilemma #4: The student seems lazy and uncooperative

"Help me find a way to present materials in an interesting way and keep classroom control in a large class setting."

"I need help motivating students to accept responsibility."

"I need ways to build character in my students, instill morals and values . . . you know, wake them up to life."

Classroom solution #4

Tie the information that needs to be taught in class to the lives of the students. Step into their world and live the morals and values you want them to adopt in the classroom. If at first they don't respond, persevere—peacefully and respectfully.

It would be quite helpful if teachers did not have to take on the parental responsibilities of building good moral character and teaching responsibility to the youth of today in their classrooms, but that's not realistic. We could try and place responsibility on parents who are not involved and who do not want to be involved—only to become more frustrated. We could continue to place certain students in alternative settings, have them return, and repeat the cycle by sending them back at their first mishap. We could continue to do all of these things with the challenging students and then continue to wonder why the strategies are not working. Or, we could try something different that requires a different way of thinking and reacting like the teacher in the following story.

Jack

Jack, a sophomore in high school, had joined a gang in his freshman year. When Mr. Williams, his history teacher, saw him almost get in trouble for wrestling in the cafeteria once during lunch time, he told him later that day in class that it was too bad he did not use his "energy" more productively because he certainly had great academic ability. Seeing that Jack was intrigued by his statement, Mr. Williams continued to tell Jack about how the wrestling team was in need of some new members. Jack thought Mr. Williams was just being sarcastic until he said he would talk to the coach with Jack the next day after school. Jack was on time for the meeting, and the coach asked him to join the team. When Mr. Williams came to his first match, Jack felt very important and waved to Mr. Williams. As a few weeks went by, Mr. Williams noticed that Jack was dressing differently and acting more positive in class. His grades improved and so did his attitude.

What happened between Jack and Mr. Williams that encouraged motivation and productivity? Mr. Williams showed an interest in Jack as a person. Mr. Williams was willing to look past the disruptive behavior and try something different. It has been my experience that many times disruptive adolescents will change their behavior when they feel that adults are purposefully watching for positive behaviors. If the students perceive that the adults are trying to catch them being "bad", they will gladly fulfill the prophecy. When adolescents respect the adult who respects them and takes the time to help in a sincere and genuine manner without confrontation and demands, they respond.

It works. Don't give up until it does.

Classroom dilemma #5: The student is falling behind in his school work and nothing I do will motivate him

"Some students just quit working late in the year. They don't realize that they have to keep their grades up so that they can move to the next grade level."

"He makes high test grades and low homework grades. Sometimes he won't even turn in the homework even when I saw him do it the previous day at school. He has to become responsible or I will have to fail him."

Classroom solution #5

Watch for times when the student does the school work. Look at the grade book and notice which assignments were completed on time and ask the student, "How were you able to do that assignment?" Talk to other teachers who teach the same student and ask for times when he does his school work.

The next case study illustrates the importance of suspending our beliefs about students who fall behind and neglect their school work It is easy to misinterpret a child's misbehavior as rebellious, defiant, or lazy. Solution-focused questions can assist us more readily in uncovering the times when these descriptions do not happen, and lead us directly to the solution.

Please slow down ... I'm not ready to be gifted yet: A case study

At ten years of age, Justin had experienced more than the average fourth grader. An attractive child, he often modeled for an agency on the weekends and spent his spare time traveling with his grandfather, a pilot. School had always gone well for him until his fourth-grade year. He began having trouble concentrating in class and began falling behind in his assignments. It was October of the new school year. He was attending the same school that he had attended since kindergarten and seemed happy enough. He just could not seem to make it through the full day of school without going to the school  nurse with a stomachache. He would go to the school nurse and complain that he was sick. The nurse would then take his temperature and, when he had no fever, would release him back to class. Justin, however, did not want to go back to class and the situation repeatedly resulted in his mom being called at least three times per week. The vice principal suggested that Justin talk to someone.

As I began to talk to Justin, I learned that the "sickness" had begun after he had run track for a school function. As he made his second lap around the field, he began wheezing and having difficulty breathing. A parent in the stands recognized that he was having trouble breathing and rushed to him on the field where Justin collapsed, heaving with each breath. Later at the emergency room, his mother and father learned that Justin had had an asthma attack. Since he had never had asthma, his parents were surprised, yet were completely supportive of the doctor's advice and Justin's determination to not return to any school activity, particularly track for a while.

Justin never seemed to fully recover. As the weeks began to go by after the accident, Justin began to call home more from school and complain of more stomachaches. After repeated doctor visits, his mother began to fear that Justin had developed anxiety attacks from his bad experience at the track field; she was sure that his aversion to being outside was directly related. As I talked to Justin, I was interested in when the stomachaches began and also what time of the day they were occurring in school. If they were related to the track incident, I would go that direction. If they were not related, I needed to know the times when he was stomachache-free. Those times would give me more information about what was going okay in his life. Those would be Justin's solutions.

LM: Justin, take me back to a time when the stomachaches weren't causing you so much of a problem.

Justin: It was before I fell at the track meet.

LM: Okay. Tell me, when is it that the stomachaches seem to happen most and bother you the most?

Justin: They usually happen about 1:30 in the afternoon in Ms. Hobbs's class. She's my new reading teacher this year.

LM: So you are saying that you go from 8:30 to 1:30 without any stomachaches?

Justin: Yes.

LM: What is it about your morning classes that help to keep the stomach-aches away?

Justin: I don't know. I just like my teacher, I guess. Her name is Ms. Livingston. She goes slower than Ms. Hobbs and she makes the work more fun. I have lots of friends in that class, too.

LM: What happens, then, when you walk into Ms. Hobbs's class at 1:30?

Justin: [squirming in his chair] "Oh, boy. Well, in that class there is so much work. She gives us lots of assignments in there. I have to go home and do so much homework … it's one of those faster classes. You know, where they think you can do more work because you're smart.

Justin's Mom: He was placed in an accelerated classroom this year because he did so well on his achievement tests. She does give a lot of homework but she seems to think that he has lots of potential.

Justin: But, Mom, it really brings me down because I can't go out and play after school. Instead, I worry about doing all of this homework when I get home. I don't like Ms. Hobbs's class. I wish I was back in Ms. Livingston's class all day like I was last year.

LM: Let's do something here, Justin. I want you to think of these stomachaches as 'troubles,' okay?

Justin: Okay.

LM: They are troubles that are keeping you from staying at school and being happy at school.

Justin: Okay.

LM: Let's say that your mom calls the school and asks for you to be placed back in Ms. Livingston's class. What would I see you doing during your school day when you had Ms. Livingston for the whole day?

Justin: I would be so much happier. I would be staying in her class all day and I would probably not have these stomachaches. I mean, troubles.

Justin's mom requested that her son be removed from the accelerated program for the remainder of the school year. She said that she would reconsider his being placed in the accelerated program the next year. While the school was reluctant, they did comply with Justin's mom's request. Justin returned to talk to me two weeks later.

LM: What's been going better for you since I've seen you?

Justin: I have not had any troubles.

LM: Really! What have you done to stop them?

Justin: Well, I changed classes and it's so much easier to do my work at school. I don't get all frustrated with all of the homework. I don't have to take too much stuff home and do a lot of work at home.

LM: Wow. You are something. So you are saying that there have not been any trips to the nurse?

Justin: Only one day … until my mom got me switched from Ms. Hobbs's class into Ms. Livingston's class. Things have been fine ever since.

On the road to understanding the challenging student

Justin's unfortunate accident could have easily been identified as the incident that caused him to begin performing poorly in school. To focus more on finding out what was wrong with Justin might have increased the chances that he would see himself as an *anxious person*. Then, Justin's system at school or at home could have catered to his anxiety and made things worse by attempting to solve the problem for him. Instead, Justin told me new information in very simple terms. When he was placed in a classroom that moved too rapidly, he was frustrated and felt incompetent since he was unable to finish his work. His teacher, Ms. Hobbs, was not able to modify the work because of the accelerated class curriculum. By listening to the student, I learned that a different classroom environment, such as Ms. Livingston's, enabled Justin to be more relaxed and successful. Someday, perhaps, when Justin is more confident, he will most probably be successful in an accelerated classroom. Or maybe he will not elect to participate in such programs at all. Whatever the decision, Justin will have enormous information for his teachers to consider when placing him in a school program. As for now, Justin has completed his year without the "troubles"—has made A's and B's in the process and never went home again with a stomachache.

Suggestions for conducting competency-based conversations

The following suggestions were helpful in my assisting Justin. They are also helpful in identifying times when your students are more motivated and productive, revealing new solutions and strategies.

1. **By listening to the given language, assist the student and/or parent with identifying a goal that is relevant for him or her.**
   Goal setting is most effective for students when the goal is stated in specific, behavioral terms. "I want to pass math" is a nice goal, but needs to be more specific. A teacher can ask for a better goal by saying:

   "What grade will I see you making when you pass math. If I watched you, what would I see you doing in class or at home that would tell me you knew how to pass math?"

2. **Search for exceptions to the problem. Search for times when the problem does not occur.**

   Problems do not occur 100% of the time. If they did, most students would not make it out of bed, or from one grade to the next. The exceptions to problems give clues to solutions. Focusing on the problem gives credence to the problem's existence and can become immobilizing to the student. Help the student identify the way she has passed other classes, for example. What strategy did she use to pass math last year? What would last year's teacher say he did that helped?

3. **Assist the student/parent by creating possibilities for the problem to be solved through a redescription of complaints and exception identification.**

   Renaming a problem into a "solvable complaint" lessens hopelessness and encourages the student to see that the problem is not impossible to solve. Changing a description of "stomachache" to "troubles" sounds more promising and possible to handle. Changing a description of "failing a class" to "you're five points from passing" makes the five points not seem so impossible to achieve.

4. **Reminisce about past successes in school.**

   Looking back over times when a student was able to enjoy school or feel motivated gives relief from the "problem" at hand. This reminiscing is freeing for the moment and allows the student to dream with the teacher about future times when school is more successful. This lighter approach to problem solving builds the teacher–student relationship and suggests that success is on the way.

5. **Develop a task collaboratively with the student or parent, based on the identified exceptions to the problem.**

    It is helpful to check with the student upon task-assignment progress so the process continues to be collaborative. This teamwork against the problem lessens failure and continues to place the student in the role of the "expert". If a teacher is working with a parent, collaboration is also important since it allows the parent to be more responsible for change and suggests that she could try the same strategy with her child in the future.

The following case study of an elementary student who had difficulties turning in her homework shows another application of the previous questions to a school problem in which the teacher felt helpless.

The day that zeros didn't work anymore: A case study

Sally, age 10, refused to turn in her homework. The teacher had tried encouraging, rewarding, and punishing Sally. There were no improvements. Sally's teacher eventually found herself working harder than Sally, looking for ways to reach her student. The teacher was *problem focused*. She focused so long on what was *wrong* with Sally's academic life that Sally saw little hope herself. Her teacher had sent notes home and had consequenced Sally with zeros after several warnings, yet Sally continued to get behind in assignments. Her test scores were high but her daily grades were causing her grades to drop drastically in the third 6-week period. Frustrated, yet determined, Sally's teacher decided to try a different approach … a solution-focused approach.

Teacher: Sally, thanks for staying after class today. You know, I've been looking at my grade book and do you realize that you have turned in seven of the last ten homework assignments?

Sally: No, I didn't.

Teacher: That says a lot about you, Sally. It's now December, and when I looked back to the first of the year, I noticed that you had turned in all of the assignments except for only a few in the first three months. Your grades were high. You are such a good student. I am quite impressed with your past record.

Sally: [silent but curious]

Teacher: I'm a little sad for you, though, because when you forget to turn in your homework sometimes, your grades don't show what a good student you really are. I wonder, what is different on the days when you *do* turn in the homework?

Sally: Sometimes I write down the assignments and then I remember to do them at home. Sometimes I forget to write them down in class so I can't do them.

Teacher: According to my grade book, you turned in almost all of your assignments early in the fall. How did you remember *then* to write down the assignments?

Sally: [thinking for a few minutes] I think it was when I sat next to the blackboard where you always wrote down the assignments. I always copied them when you reminded us to do it before school ended.

Teacher: Are you saying that sitting next to the board helped that much ... and that my reminding you helped?

Sally: I guess so. In my music class I always remember to practice my flute because the teacher gives us the practice sheets for our parents to sign. I have it everyday. I guess I need reminders and to see it written down.

Teacher: What do you think you might do for the next few days to help you remember? I'm interested in helping you get back on track like you were before. It must have been fun for you to show everyone what a good student you were.

Sally: Yes. My mom was happy then. Maybe I could sit up close to the board again?

Teacher: I'll be glad to let you sit up close again. Over the next few days I will be looking forward to seeing you turn in your homework like you used to. I will be glad to remind you to write things down as well. Could you write me a note to keep here on my desk so I don't forget?

The following steps were taken by Sally's teacher:

- Sally's teacher looked back at Sally's success and mentioned the success first, implying that Sally was capable of turning in her homework. She presented what she *did* do well rather than what she was deficient in doing.

- The teacher suggested to Sally that she obviously knew how to turn in her homework and asked her what she had done before that worked for her, making Sally the expert. She wanted Sally to become more competent and she thought that if she (the teacher) made any suggestions, she would be robbing Sally of feeling competent. When Sally came up with the solution, it was her solution, and the strategies were simple and appropriate for Sally's age.

- The teacher took Sally's suggestions and told her that she would be watching for Sally's success. This "set the stage" for Sally to come through as her teacher perceived her. Say "when you are showing everyone what a good student you are" is different from saying "I want to see you bring up your grades because you are capable." The first phrase gives Sally all the credit; the second phrase deduces that Sally must please the teacher. Sally is more likely to continue changing behaviors when the motivation is intrinsic.

- Together, Sally and her teacher looked for "exceptions" to the times when she did her homework. "Exceptions" are the times when the problem is less of a problem. If the teacher had confronted Sally and told her that she was in danger of failing the class, the opportunity for Sally to solve her own problem might not have come so easily, since the current situation was so grim. Instead, focusing on when Sally had passed, opened up past successes that became new tasks.

Sally began turning in her homework again and raised her grades. Her mother called Sally's teacher to inquire what was going on at school, since Sally was in such a good mood thereafter when she returned home each day. Sally's teacher briefly described to Sally's mom what she had learned about when Sally turned in her homework best. From then on, whenever Sally's teacher suspected that Sally was getting off track, she simply talked with her about how she had been "on track" before and Sally took charge again.

Classroom dilemma #6: The student will not take responsibility for her actions

"Some of my students disrupt the class and never take responsibility for their actions. I have tried sending them to the office but sometimes they just skip school."

"My third grade class has a girl who talks constantly and keeps others around her from doing their work. I have called her parents and kept her after school but she still talks too much."

"A student got involved in a fight during my class and was suspended. When she came back she still had her attitude and it almost happened again."

Classroom solution #6

Help the student change her reputation with those who see her as irresponsible. When the student blames someone else, agree that it was an uncomfortable situation and then ask the student to tell you what it would take to avoid a similar situation in the future.

"It's Someone Else's Fault"— Encouraging Responsibility and Discouraging Blame

Here are suggestions for thinking about and helping students who wish to change the minds of those who see them as irresponsible.

When students are accused of wrongdoings, they often become defensive and sometimes respond by blaming someone else. Students, especially adolescents, often feel vulnerable to the expectations of others (parents or teachers) and respond with blame to feel less rejected. Over the years as an educator, I have observed countless colleagues who attempted to get students to "see the light" through well-meant criticism, confrontation, or punishment to little or no avail. Their well-meant strategies did not work, so, instead of being helpful, the students and teachers ended up in power struggles where, hierarchically speaking, the teachers "won," as the student, ignoring the discussion, said just enough to warrant punishment.

In keeping with the solution-focused idea of "creating an environment where people can experience competency" (Durrant, 1993), I have found it helpful to think of the following basic beliefs when presented with a student who feels "persecuted" and needs a way to change his or her reputation.

Brainstorming "justice" with students

1. Aligning with the student in his or her complaint and pursuit of justice will lessen resistance.

   "It must be really tough to hear what Mr. Scott says about you so often—no wonder you want things better for you. How will you know when things are better for you in his class? What will I see you doing when that happens?" (joining and goal setting)

2. Assuming that the student has a valid argument and that the argument is a defense mechanism, not an attempt to defeat someone, will "normalize" the student's view.

   "I certainly understand why you're upset and why your mom is worried. Can you tell me times when you don't feel quite so upset? What are you doing during those times that helps you to stay calm and not be so upset by this 'problem'? " (searching for exceptions to the presenting problem)

3. Wondering out loud what new behaviors might change the "blamed" person's mind about the student will stop the blame and place responsibility on the student.

   "I wonder what Mr. Scott might see you doing in the near future that would really change his mind about you. I've got this feeling that he really hasn't seen the person I'm meeting with today. You seem so concerned about school ... what do you think it would take to get Mr. Scott off your back? Have you gotten him to lay off before? How did you do this?" (further exception identification/beginnings of task development)

4. Assuming that the student has accomplished such a needed, convincing maneuver before, to be successful in other similar situations will encourage his or her chance at success again.

   "You know, this is the first time I've met with you this year ... that tells me you have known how to keep the teachers happy for ___ (months, weeks). How have you done this? What would your other teachers say you do in their classes that works? Based on what you just described to me, what do you think you might try just for a few days in Mr. Scott's class to get him to back off?" (task development)

Working with the negative-thinking student

Noticing *exceptions* is an integral part of what the solution-focused teacher does. As a teacher begins to use the ideas in this book, he or she is often surprised that students and parents become very quiet and solemn when they are asked, "How did you do that?" Many students and parents have experienced years of being told *what's wrong* by

well-meaning teachers. This context also gave them reason to *ask the teachers to solve the problem, since they were the ones complaining about performance.* Our world is a problem-focused one, focusing on less-than-successful times. As with any other new approach, skill-building takes time. It is helpful for a teacher to think of how she has implemented other approaches before or how he has explained a new approach with a parent. Perhaps duplicating the "Brainstorming New Motivational Strategies" worksheet, making note cards, or displaying a short version of the guidelines given earlier in Chapter Three may give confidence to the beginning solution-focused teacher.

It would not be fair, however, to mention that some people are simply determined to focus only on problems—how bad things are in their lives—and are quite resistant to noticing anything besides the problem at hand. In keeping with the basic solution-focused philosophy, *nothing is 100%,* and sometimes different approaches need to be taken to approach students who see things particularly negatively. If this occurs, a solution-focused teacher can *cooperate with the problem focus (by seeing it negatively with them),* since it is their *world view,* and say:

"You know, this does sound really horrible."

"When is it the absolute worst?"

"On a scale of 1-10 with a '10' meaning it totally takes over your life and a '1' meaning you are in control, where are you now?"

If the student describes a number lower than 10, ask:

"How have you been able to keep it from being a '10'?"

"What would it take for you to move down only one step?"

When students or parents are stuck, they only see the worst. These questions respectfully align with the person's negative view and help him or her to realize that things aren't so bad as he or she perceived.

Concluding comments

As teachers, we hold in our hands the tools to construct or deconstruct our students. Each time we talk with a student, compliment them, or help them to solve a problem, we become coauthors in their lives. Today's students bring a collage of problems and concerns with them to school and sometimes rely on us to process their concerns. If their families turn their backs on them and we do the same, for whom will they reach?

Their needs are still there. It's time to realize that as teachers, our jobs are evolving into more than instructors of curriculum. We are now trainers for life with apprentices that come willing—and sometimes unwilling—to our lessons. Our approach must be different to win over the unwilling. However, those who are succeeding today say that the solution is not so difficult and insurmountable as it appears. Inside each student is a person who needs inspiration, respect, and dignity, just like ourselves. The solution-focused teacher receives his or her dose of inspiration and respect from the students who blossom from the dignity he or she possesses.

"There are two educations. One should teach us how to make a living and the other how to live."

—James Truslow Adams

Chapter Three Practice Exercise

Creating Possibilities: Acknowledging Strengths Through Language

(Make five copies of the note below. Give three to your closest colleagues and two to students you admire. Tell them you are trying to concentrate on making things "work" better for you in school. Ask them to fill out the form and return it to you. In return, tell them what you have always appreciated about them.)

Date: _____

Dear: _____,

I am interested in how you see my performance here at school. Your comments are very important to me, for I respect and treasure your opinion.

Below, please list what you think I do well here at school. It is my hope that your ideas will tell me what I need to keep doing more of.

Sincerely,

_____

Comments:

_____

_____

_____

_____

_____

_____

_____

_____

_____

_____

Formula First Session Task for Students and Teachers*

For the new few days, notice times when: (circle one) teacher, student, parent moves away from the behaviors that brought you here today. Write down what you saw him or her do that was different.

_____

_____

_____

_____

_____

_____

_____

Notice times in the classroom with (teacher) when you don't find yourself giving in to the behaviors that brought you here today. Write them here.

_____

_____

_____

_____

_____

_____

_____

_____

_____

_____

Next meeting date: _____

*Adapted from De Shazer, 1985.

Brainstorming Solutions for Parent Conferences *(continued)*

Student Name: _____   Teacher Name: _____

Goals of Teacher for the Student:

1. _____

   _____

2. _____

   _____

3. _____

   _____

Teacher Observations of Times when the Goal(s) Occur More Often (exceptions):

Times when the student performs or behaves more successfully.

1. _____

   _____

2. _____

   _____

3. _____

   _____

Goal of Parent(s) and Student

Student and parent's description of gradual goal achievement for the next week.

1. _____

   _____

2. _____

   _____

3. _____

   _____

Brainstorming Solutions for Parent Conferences *(continued)*

Times When Parents Have Noticed the Goals Occurring More (exceptions):

Parent's description of more successful teaching situations that worked better for his/her son or daughter.

1. _____

    _____

2. _____

    _____

3. _____

    _____

Strategies to Promote Success in the Classroom:

Using the two lists of exceptions identified, describe strategies for the student, parent, and teacher for the next week.

1. _____

    _____

2. _____

    _____

3. _____

    _____

Chapter Four
The Exceptional School Program
Changing Teacher–Student Relationships

"Better than a thousand days of diligent study is one day with a great teacher."

—Japanese Proverb

The exceptional educators

A fictional case study for the future

The time on the digital clock read 8:10 a.m. Ms. Rodriguez was busy putting finishing touches on her sixth-grade classroom. In 20 minutes, a school-appointed colleague would arrive with a camera and she wanted to create just the right impression and environment for her students and herself to have a good morning together. The science lab was ready for the individual groups that worked so well last week. The math center was filled with toothpicks for the morning experiment. Touching and feeling items kept the interest level with these "regular" students. The library passes were ready for just the right moment when a student was curious about an idea. Ms. Rodriguez knew the importance of spontaneity. Finally, her morning story from the daily news was on her desk. She routinely talked about the news with her students and had them recall "their" news as well. This lively 10-minute discussion always seemed to convey the true feelings for her students and get them off to a good start with something different each day. She checked her lesson plans and made sure that today's plan was different from yesterday, full of intermittent stimuli and in sync with what she and her students had decided worked for the first four months of the school year. She was ready.

In Ms. Rodriguez's school district, the administration had begun a project three years ago that had enhanced teaching styles and encouraged motivation among its educators. Elected by their individual schools, teachers were chosen as "exceptional teachers" who consistently created an environment in which students felt competent, successful, and excited about learning. The teachers were nominated by students and chosen by their colleagues. Instead of awarding certificates at the end of the school year, the district chose this route that benefited all of its staff members districtwide. The district chose from several volunteer teachers who were handy with video cameras to videotape the "exceptional teachers" each semester and the videotapes were played to similar grade level/subject matter teachers in the district at bi-yearly inservices. This method of illustrating "what works with students" was welcomed by the teachers, who gained hands-on knowledge of their colleagues' expertise, and felt they were not being given information by an outsider. Instead, a teacher in the same situations as they, with the same struggles and frustrations, showed his or her way of creating a competent atmosphere. Typically, the "exceptional teacher" accompanied the inservice and explained his or her strategies. Discussions were held after the tape was shown and collaborative conversations developed.

A new approach to team meetings

Upon leaving the inservice meetings, attending teachers held weekly "team meetings" in their separate buildings, where they discussed utilizing some of the ideas they saw on videotape and added their own personal styles. In their team meetings, which now lasted a maximum of 30 minutes each week, ideas were exchanged about what worked in certain assignments (each was required to bring at least one). Instead of complaining about students, each team teacher brought up concerns about particular students. The team members then discussed, from their personal experience, how they managed to cooperate with the student, helping that student to behave or be responsible in class. The team of teachers, who all taught Student A, for example, might decide upon a strategy to use during the next week. They also might decide to notice when Student A did better. The teachers discussed their findings in the next meeting, always beginning their meeting with "What's going better for this student?"

Three principles that will work for your students

In today's busy classrooms, weaknesses and struggles become the focus as teachers try to create environments for learning in environments that often must be quite negative and problem-focused to keep order and control. While well meant, these programs ignore the strengths of students as teachers try to keep classroom order. It almost seems difficult to decide who suffers more: the students, unnoticed for their strengths due to their misbehavior, or the teachers, burned out from being disciplinarians with little energy left for creative teaching. Caught in a difficult situation, many teachers respond negatively towards their students due to stress and the constant need to be in charge. The students, in turn, respond defensively; thus, learning becomes a scarce commodity.

Developmentally, children and adolescents thrive on *acceptance*, *validation*, and *structure*. When the school program centers around assertive discipline, the teachers' and administrators' reactions to the students typically happens when the students misbehave. While many teachers praise their "behaving" students, those students who misbehave miss out on praise and perpetually get attention negatively. While some would say that it is the student's fault for not receiving praise ("If she would only behave, I would praise her"), often the negative behaviors occur *because* the student does not feel accepted, validated, and successful. If you have ever failed repeatedly to achieve something, you know how difficult it is to motivate yourself toward trying one more time. The same occurs for students. My work as a teacher, school counselor, and family therapist has taught me how these three principles make a difference in motivating people to change their lives. Because of the changes I've witnessed when these ingredients are present, I continue to implement and suggest them. However, today's teacher is under tremendous pressure and can easily forget to accept, validate, and expect structure when students seem to be out of control. However, like any new habit, once the habit pays off, it becomes easier to do. If you have a student in your classroom who always seems to misbehave, experiment with the following ideas for one week.

1. Tell the student that you would like to do an experiment. Tell her that during the next week you want to change your mind about her behavior because you think that you have not been able to see what a fine student she really is. Tell her you will write down daily the things she does well and would like to send a note home with her on Friday to tell her parents what you noticed during the week.

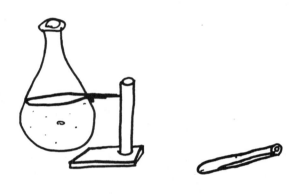

2. Watch! Notice how she answers in class sometimes, how she finishes some of her class work, how she refrains from talking slightly.

3. Observe what you do in the classroom that helps her to pay attention more often, refrain from talking, do her work. Does she respond better when you circulate more and stand by her desk when she talks? Does she finish her work when you walk by and compliment her on anything, even her hair or dress? Does she seem to answer in class when you call on her and compliment her even when she is incorrect?

4. Send a note home on Friday. Even if the student does not make a wealth of changes during the week, write her parents and tell them that you are determined to help their child/adolescent feel better about herself and that during the next week you will be watching for what she does well in class. Tell them it is your new strategy to bring out the best in their offspring.

We can't wait any longer

When schools *do* offer the three principles of acceptance, validation, and structure to their methods of approaching and instructing students, the students succeed and their resistance is low. The key is, *how* do we show acceptance, validation, and structure? Past theories of educational discipline techniques and behavior modification approaches *waited* for students to prove to educators that they knew how to act in school. However, in today's schools—volatile with peer pressure and less parental involvement—rarely do educators support such an environment. Maybe it's time to do more than place stars on good papers. Maybe it's time to notice when students pass or come near passing and ask them, *"How did you do that?"* Solution-focused teachers who work in very volatile schools report that the students who once flinched when they touched their paper, now look to them as nurturing. They report that teaching is more satisfying and their students are succeeding with less prompting. In a junior high school in Texas, the principal told me that he makes it a daily occurrence to spontaneously visit classrooms in his building. At first his teachers were taken back when he strolled into their classrooms and sat down in a student desk, but when they saw their students increase their performance, they began to invite him in. In that same school, the principal, Mr. Darrell Sneed, created many new clubs for students to belong to. He told me research has claimed that when students are involved in extracurricular activities, they feel more involved and therefore perform better in the classroom. Again, validation, acceptance, and structure win.

Learning to cooperate with students

The ideas in Chapter Four are suggested as a means to help educators become flexible *within a structure that encourages students to feel competent.* Where else is there a better place to encourage competency than in our schools? As we look into effective classrooms around the world, we often find teachers who are structured yet are cooperating with their students' differences in various ways—whether the encouragement comes from a teacher who praises her students with words or notes of appreciation, or a teacher who teams up a bright, but shy student with another equally shy student with similar attributes. The teacher or counselor who notices what her students do well and then allows, encourages, and expects more of it, *often sees it.*

When I was a junior high Art teacher over a decade ago, students were often placed in my classroom when they had disrupted and sabotaged other electives. Apparently, the administrators in my school (and other schools) had too much faith in me for they seemed to feel that these difficult students simply needed a chance to be creative. While I have to confess that I did not agree with them, I rarely did have problems with these "difficult" students. In fact, they did so well, I began asking for the troubled kids because I loved seeing them change and view themselves so successfully. What went on in the Art class was: structure, validation, *fun*, and acceptance. When the "difficult" students (whom I referred to as *challenging*, not difficult) began to act up, I found something I knew they could do … whether it was putting up new Art projects for others to see in the hallway, handing out supplies, or cleaning up around the weaving loom. They often hung out around my desk asking for more tasks. At one point I had several classes of

40 students each—we scarcely had enough chairs but we had fun and very few problems. Cooperating with who they were lessened resistance and encouraged learning.

Acceptance centers on listening for what the student needs and aligning with those needs. Acceptance occurs every time a teacher assists a student in reaching a specific goal. It occurs as teachers notice and verbalize what a student does well, and adds the ingredient of curiosity:

"Wow, I agree, it is time to get me off your back. What do you think you can do to accomplish that for just today?"

Notice times when students do *something you can accept*. Tell them about it pronto! Acceptance lessens resistance. Less resistance is a solution-focused teacher's best friend.

It's just the language that's different

Cooperating with students means validating them. When I acknowledged that Joey had the ability to stop a fight by being polite initially, and then asked him to do more of that with his mother, I validated his strategy. Learning to cooperate with students and help them to realize their competencies, requires that teachers, counselors, and administrators perceive the students differently, and look more closely at what *they can do*. If we perceive a child as hyperactive, traumatized, sexually abused, angry, or depressed, we tend to react with kid gloves and thereby perpetuate the problem. More than one student (and adult) has told me *why* they cannot do a certain behavior. These explanations become, as Brad Keeney (1994) said, "barbed wire fences". If someone walks up to you this afternoon and remarks that you look as if you have had a tough day when you, in fact, felt it was a great day, you may have a tendency to look twice when you pass the nearest mirror and the rest of your day may appear different to you.

The description of the behavior is often the same ... the language is just different. However, a pathological description is not validating, only informative. How would you like yourself to be described? Sure, people become sad, upset, and often act out their frustrations. They also get over such feelings for the most part. To label a student as having a *conduct disorder* sticks a description on her forehead that is hard to lose. Talking in problem-focused language such as that perpetuates the problem. Thinking about a student as having a conduct disorder prohibits you from seeing anything else. The solution-focused teacher, however, is more interested in solutions than problems so she puts the label aside so that she can reach and teach the student.

> *By the time a problem comes to the attention of a counselor, it will have attracted a variety of explanations and ideas about what needs to happen to it* (Durrant, 1993, p. 6).

Structure can be freedom

Creating an environment in which students can feel competent does not mean we lower the expectations and become free spirited teachers who allow the throes of creativity to take over our classrooms and create havoc. Quite contrarily, this approach encourages structure, for within that structure is safety and stability. Structure means that students can depend on the teacher's consistency and her creativity. If someone asked you to begin a new job today, and the only instruction was to "get the job done by 5:00 or you're fired", most of us would find ourselves scrambling for some type of structure or instruction and that very scrambling would keep us from being as successful as we could be. Students experience the same trauma. It is important for students to experience creative lesson plans and classroom rules that are in place and consistently followed. The rules are also of the type that work … and are enforceable. The rules are also flexible, within a structure that does not waiver. For example, notice the following scenario of an exceptional solution-focused teacher.

Case study

Mrs. Thomas began the history lesson by spontaneously dividing up the class into four groups. Group A was a rather advanced group; Group B, an average group; Group C, a creative group; and Group D, a group of students who struggled with reading. She asked the question: "Who knows something about World War II?" One hand went up out of the entire class. "Ken, what can you tell us?" Ken began to describe the weaponry he learned about from his grandfather. He said he had developed a particular interest in the weapons since he was in fourth grade. He had read several books and told the class a few ideas.

"Who else knows something about World War II?" The rest of the class reported small instances from a chapter they were assigned to read last night, but generally, the class was not ready for a discussion. Mrs. Thomas assigned various topics within the World War II assignment. Group A was to study the economic consequences; Group B, the rebuilding after the war; Group C, a story/script for enacting what it might have been like for families whose loved ones fought the war. Mrs. Thomas and Group D read the chapter together, Mrs. Thomas taking a place amongst her students, saying, "I need to read this chapter again, too." The student who acknowledged his knowledge of World War II was released from group work since he knew about the subject of weapons. Mrs. Thomas told him, "You are obviously familiar with World War II. I don't want to bore you. I'd like you to go to the library and study some more and then present us all with a presentation on weapons, complete with pictures, in a week. You may use the library each class period this week."

In Mrs. Thomas's class, structure was freedom to feel competent and behave as such. Mrs. Thomas was confident in her ability to manage the class and take a position of inquiry instead of lecturing. By asking the class initially "Who knows something about World War II?", she invited student participation and proceeded with identifying and grouping similarly competent students together without distinguishing them from each other.

Student referrals are opportunities for collaboration

Invariably, most teachers are successful at maintaining many tasks and situations during their school day. Perhaps the teacher who feels frustrated with a particular student may not notice the other 26 children she manages well in her classroom. The acting-out student gets her attention first and can set a negative tone for everyone else. If the focus on the student continues, the teacher might take out her frustrations on the rest of the class—and acceptance, validation, and structure fly out the window. The Teacher Referral Form included in this chapter, grew from the comments of teachers who began to list exceptions instead of problems on paper when visiting with their students. Many of the teachers often found themselves overwhelmed with misbehaving students and were expected to perform miracles by their administrators. Most teachers who have used solution-focused ideas have found their students to be less resistant as they avidly wrote down the students' exceptions. The teachers also found that many parents began to cooperate more often when they *saw* the Teacher Referral Form, and perceived that the school was more interested in growth and competency building with their child than punishing the child.

In typical school situations, students are referred to counselors or administrators by teachers who are frustrated with students and expect the counselor or administrator to "solve the student's problem". Such a process relinquishes responsibility from the interactive parties and keeps the teacher–student relationship from changing. Instead, the counselor or administrator is asked to become the primary resource for both teacher and student, often resulting in further confusion. While momentary resolution may happen between *counselor/administrator* and student, nothing changes between the teacher and student, encouraging relapse. If anything, things worsen between the teacher and the student after the teacher refers the student for punishment. Often, the student seeks revenge upon return to the classroom and will carry out his or her feelings with more misbehavior. Besides, the third party was not present during the problematic times and only knows to represent the teacher's best interest so the school keeps a united front. Nice, but what happens to the student? He or she is left on his or her own to come up with solutions—and the student's inexperience in problem solving inhibits carrying out successful strategies without a better relationship with his teacher.

Keeping it between teacher and student

It seems more realistic and helpful for the teacher *and* the student to talk privately and develop solutions to *their* concerns without becoming defensive with each other. The

 school counselor can also be helpful by becoming the consultant to the teacher—*not* the mediator. In many situations, the counselor is asked for answers to *why* a student behaves as he or she does. Is a divorce occurring at home? Has the child been sexually abused? Is there a student–student conflict? Many of these viable questions may hold answers but are not feasible in assisting a child to behave in class *currently*, nor are the answers always accurate as to *why* the behavior is occurring. In some problem-focused approaches, questions that search for reasons behind negative behaviors assume that the student has a serious problem and may provoke resistance and prejudice regarding what the student is capable of achieving due to the problems. The blame is placed on the student and assumes failure on the student's behalf, or the parents assume it is the school's fault, that the school program is not motivating their child. School should be a place where students learn responsibility for their actions and also learn alternatives. A school counselor or teacher can do nothing about an impending divorce, nor does he or she have the knowledge to deal with the issues arising from sexual abuse. Learning *why* humans behave as they do may be fascinating but it does not give us clues as to changing them. In fact, there have never been any research or studies anywhere that proved knowing *why* something happened helped people to change. Those who truly wanted their lives to be different simply changed out of necessity, desire, or opportunity.

Referring to what works

The Teacher Referral Form on page 107 was designed to take the responsibility of teacher–student conflict and place it back in the hands of the teacher and student involved. It is particularly helpful in the following situations:

1. The teacher completes the form for a few days *before* talking to the student about her concern. The student is notified by his teacher of the referral form so that he is challenged to show new behaviors to his teacher. This new context of "I'm watching for your good side" is attractive to many students who feel as if they have been focused on negatively.

2. When a teacher has had little success in offering consequences to a challenging student, he can show the form to the student and tell her that he is interested in watching for what she is successful at during the next few classes. The solution-focused teacher is more interested in the *times when the negative behavior/problem is not existing* and challenges his students to help him notice. It takes time to look beyond the fog of problems towards exceptions. Watch out for puzzled looks from students! Persevere.

3. When a team of teachers is determined to help a student change behaviors, meeting with the student and showing him the Teacher Referral Form as an opportunity to help the teachers see how he learns and behaves best takes the student off guard. The student's strategies are suddenly no longer justified. He is vulnerable and

Teacher Referral Form

Name of Student _____ Grade _____ Date _____

Dear Teacher,

Below, please list the times when you notice _____ doing *well* in class. These observations will be very helpful to this student and his or her parents as you talk about some solutions to the concern you have.

Please be as specific as possible; for example, "Suzie did well in class today when she chose to sit by herself while completing her assignment."

1. _____

2. _____

3. _____

4. _____

5. _____

_____

Teacher Signature

Copy sent to parents?   Yes   No   (circle)

challenged when he begins to feel accepted and validated. At first, he may appear resistant, but a continuance of this *new attitude* by his teachers will lessen the probability that he will continue acting out. The project will require that the teachers verbally remind the student that they are watching. It is also helpful in this situation that one teacher be the spokesperson for the team and that each teacher keeps his or her solution-focused stance while the team presents the project to the student.

The map will tell you where to go

As the teacher completes the referral form and begins to identify exceptions (times when misbehavior or unsuccessful actions do *not* happen) to the student's behavior or academic life, two new behaviors emerge. First, the teacher begins to notice times when the problem isn't so prevalent and, as a result, may see and feel differently towards the student, thus reacting differently towards her. Second, as the teacher reacts differently to the student, the student may begin to behave more appropriately in response. There is a big difference in telling a student what a teacher noticed her doing well and telling her what she already knows is going poorly. This philosophy is metaphorical to that of reading a map. Maps have many routes to follow to reach many destinations. The scenic route winds through small towns, while the freeway moves more quickly through a direct route. Both routes get to the same destination. The solution-focused teacher is the travel guide, offering suggestions and observing scenery from the *exceptions* noticed along the route. Schools rarely have time for the scenic route, yet solution-focused ideas provide the freeway. Instead of berating a problem and figuring out who's to blame, the model bypasses such "barbed wire fences" along the way and jumps over them toward more pleasant pastures, believing there are no boundaries once one is thinking toward solutions.

Ideas to remember while developing student solutions

The act of completing the referral form is in itself an intervention. As the student talks with the solution-focused teacher and hears the exceptions written down by his or her teacher, the student should learn three things:

1. **The school is on my side and teachers are here to assist me in being successful.** When schools approach children and adolescents with confrontation and as "problems", they behave as such and respond rebelliously. When students are approached in a firm manner yet are asked to self-evaluate themselves, they are given the chance to prove that they can behave differently. When we cooperate with students, teachers, and parents, we lessen resistance. I like to think of teachers as travel guides or consultants as they fill out the referral form. They get to point out the scenery that the student has missed while in distress.

2. **It doesn't seem so hard to change as I thought.** Students tend to blame others — it is, after all, much easier to blame someone else for our failures and to deny being responsible for changing the outcome. Aligning with students and asking them "What do you see yourself doing that will keep you from getting yourself off track (in trouble) in my classroom?" will encourage a student to make changes. Asking "What do you think it will take for you to avoid getting into a fight today at lunch?" assumes that the student is capable and responsible. "What do you suppose you can do to raise your history grade five points during the next week?" assumes that the student can raise her grade and in a realistic way.

3. **Maybe I'm not so helpless as I thought I was.** Students who progress to the next grade year after year (or even if they are held back once or twice) are at least successful in being promoted. That is an exception. The elementary student who goes three days a week without being sent to the office for fighting is behaviorally competent three days a week. Those three days are exceptions. Pointing out her ability to stay out of trouble three days a week builds competent feelings and reinforces her ability to do more of what works on those days. For a high school junior who is an outstanding football player, learning new geometry formulas may present too many new challenges, leaving him to feel lost. By asking him how he might have handled learning the complicated plays from his football coach, he begins to think of himself as competent. Many of us have ways of handling situations that fall into various categories: stress, anger, worry, frustration, new job, new relationships, too much to do, and so on. By helping students to realize that they have already accomplished similar feats in other contexts, we help them to formulate new and competent beliefs in themselves.

Follow-up to reinforce!

The follow-up conversations after the initial one reinforces to the student that the teacher is serious about observing exceptions and success.

"What's going better in class for you? I'm very interested in your ideas. Today I noticed _____ about you."

Be forewarned: Students who admit things are better may fear that such admissions are hazardous to relationships with you! (They might like the attention!) Be persistent and let your students know that you will be glad to talk to them even when the troubling times are over. David Epston from New Zealand and coauthor of *Narrative Means to Therapeutic Ends* routinely sends notes to people after he meets with them the first time. He summarizes the visit, notes his impressions, and adds compliments and tasks. This could be used for a student as follows:

Dear Shawna,

I enjoyed meeting with you today after school. I was amazed at your ability to point out times when the problem did not bother you in your other classes; you said six out of seven classes go well. I was also impressed by your plan to move to the front of the room so you are not distracted, since that apparently works well in your Algebra class as well. Good luck. Stop by several times this week to tell me how things are working. I'm pulling for you.

Mrs. Greenberg

The teacher can copy the note to Shawna and send it home with her to her parents and give a copy to the vice principal.

Included here are sample notes to copy and use to compose student letters. The first note is appropriate for the secondary student and the second note is for the elementary student.

More simple interventions for teachers

Another collaborative way that teachers can make simple interventions and motivate their students is through weekly *scaling questions*. Ellen Boehmer, a school counselor at Terrace Elementary School in Richardson, Texas, adapted scaling questions into a simple-to-use method for teachers. She duplicated a scale on 3 x 5 cards. Upon giving them to teachers of troubled students, she explained to the teacher *and* the students that "1" meant the problem was in control and "10" meant the student was in control. She suggested that the teacher and student collaborate once a week (the day of their choice) and talk about where the student was on the scale, based on their concerns. The teachers used the 3 x 5 cards to scale positive behavior, successful grades, and appropriate participation in school. The teacher simply has to ask, "How have you moved from here to here?" or, "Where would you like to be during the next week?" The sample scale and guiding questions are given here. Draw the scale on a 3 x 5 card and ask the guiding questions.

Teacher _____   Class/Grade _____

Student _____   Week of _____

_____

   1   2   3   4   5   6   7   8   9   10

You have impressed me!

Date:_____

Dear _____,

I have been observing you recently in my classroom! You have impressed me in many ways and I wanted you to know what I have noticed about you and your abilities:

_____

_____

_____

_____

_____

_____

_____

_____

As things continue to go well for you, I predict:

_____

_____

_____

_____

Thanks for being in my classroom. I am proud to be your teacher.

_____

Teacher Signature

With your approval, copies of this note can be sent to:

Wow, you are ... a super star!

Date: _____

Dear _____,

I have been watching you in class this
week. I am happy to tell you about some
of the wonderful things I have learned about you. I am proud to be your teacher.

_____

_____

_____

_____

_____

_____

_____

_____

When you keep up this great work, I think the future will be bright for you because:

_____

_____

_____

_____

Teacher Signature

I am going to give _____ a copy of this note if it is okay
with you.

Questions and ideas for elementary students

1. "On this scale are some numbers,1 through 10. The scale is like a ruler. A '1' means a problem is bothering you and keeping you stuck in my classroom. It makes you _____." (Name behaviors that keep the child from getting good citizenship grades.) "A '10' means that you are on top of the problem and it never bothers you. Where do you think you are on this scale today?"

2. "What do you think you might do just for today that would help you move up just one point?"

3. "What can I do to help you move up?"

4. "I'll talk to you on _____ so we can both see how you have moved."

Questions and ideas for secondary students

1. "Everybody gets stuck sometimes when they have lots of things going on in their lives. I know you have a lot going on, too. I want you to look at this scale for a minute. On the left is a '1' and on the right is a '10'. Suppose the '1' meant that things in this classroom are really off track ... you know, where you don't feel like you are making any progress at all. Then, suppose the '10' meant that you are totally successful in this class and you are in control totally. Where do you think you are today on this scale?"

2. "What do you think you could do just for today or tomorrow that might help you to begin moving up the scale just slightly?"

3. "What could I do?"

4. "I will talk to you on _____ so we can both see where you have moved to."

If the student makes little progress, suggest that at least he or she did not move backwards. Then ask:

"How do you explain your ability to not let things get any worse?"

If the student moves backwards one week, ask:

"How did you move up before? Let's look back and recall your strategies/actions that helped you to be more on track."

Reversing the pressure: encouraging a student to influence other students

The parent of a student asked her daughter to relay to me this wonderful intervention that occurred for her at her junior high school:

Student: I guess I had not been doing so well as I was before these last six weeks. I'd kind of gotten lazy. One day last week, all of my teachers called me into the conference room. I just knew I was in deep trouble. Instead, do you know what they said? They said they were concerned about me. They said I was a good kid and that other students really looked up to me and that I could really help them out. I was shocked. They went around the room and each of them told me something good about myself. I've never had anything like this happen at school.

LM: Wow, what else happened then?

Student: They told me my grades had dropped but they had my folder there and showed me how I had done so well early in the year. They asked me if I needed anything from them so I could improve. I couldn't believe it. It was a real trip. I told them I didn't know right away but I would think about it. They told me they were going to watch me very closely and ask me if I needed them.

LM: They must really believe in you.

Student: I guess so!

This student went from 70's to 90's in six weeks. Her mom was very impressed with the initiative of the school to call this conference with her daughter. The daughter felt a mild pressure to improve and a sense of support that she had not recognized before. The teachers who were clever enough to devise such a conference gave this student a belief in herself that she needed during the troubled time she was going through. How wise of the teachers to approach her this way ... it was respectful (no inquiries as to "what's wrong"), compassionate, and very empowering. The student felt supported and saw herself as important. The conference took ten minutes from class preparation before school one day and the results are still in effect, four months later! Focusing on when the student did well—mixed with concerns, empathy, compliments, and a plan of action—equaled student success.

Dealing with the resistant student

Webster defines *resistance* as "an organized, usually underground, movement of fighters engaged in acts of sabotage, etc., against occupying forces" (1987). Students and parents sometimes become resistant when they feel:

- blamed for a situation
- unsuitable to the person
- insecure with their abilities

- uninformed about the scope of things
- misunderstood regarding their opinion
- violated when asked to do things beyond their ability
- offended when asked to go against morals
- overwhelmed when asked to do unreasonable things
- inferior due to no cooperation from the other person

Looking into school settings, many systemic factors contribute to student resistance. Economic situations, inadequate supervision, criticism from parents, lack of acknowledgment/acceptance by teachers and peers, jealousy of peers with more advantages—plus many more—encourage resistance in many school clients. However gloomy it seems, though, the three principles apply once again: acceptance, validation, and structure.

It is sometimes difficult to notice exceptions in others as this case represents. Granted, in a violent student, failing sixth grader, or angry tenth grader, it is difficult to see competencies. The difficulties arise when the student refuses to "cooperate". When this occurs, consider that his or her behaviors serve a purpose, so do not try to change the behavior. This will lessen resistance. In other words, stepping into the school client's world view means trying to understand that the behavior we observe is necessary to the school client. I have found it helpful to ask how the negative behavior *helps* and then assist the student with "doing more of the same" only in a different manner.

LM: Don, your teacher said she sent you to talk to me because you continue to interrupt her in class. Is this correct in your point of view?

Don: Yeah, she doesn't like me and never calls on me, so why not?

LM: Does this work for you, to interrupt her constantly?

Don: Yeah, and I'm not going to stop either. She keeps on my case all the time and I'm sick of it. I'm not going to let her boss me around.

LM: Tell me, I'm curious, what does it do for you, to interrupt her?

Don: I don't know … I guess it gets her attention.

LM: Good attention or bad attention?

Don: Bad, and I don't care.

LM: How could you use your interrupting skills a little differently in class … it sounds like you're not willing to give them up.

Don: I don't know.

LM: I'm just wondering if you could interrupt Ms. Lee a little differently, you know, so she really notices you. This may take some skill, though, and some real observation on your part so that you get the maximum benefit from interrupting her. Would you be willing to try something different?

Don: Maybe.

LM: I'd like you to interrupt Ms. Lee this afternoon in class when she is explaining something to your class. Watch for precisely the exact moment when she would truly hear your interruption. You know, when she pauses, or is passing out papers. Then, I'd like you to tell her 'I need to interrupt for a minute . . .' and then ask a question about what she was explaining. This way you will interrupt her and we can both see what you accomplish. I'd like you to try this just twice this week. Is it okay with you if we write Ms. Lee a note and mention that you will be trying something different?

Don: Okay.

As the student attempts to use his or her method differently, it is helpful to inform the teacher that the student is planning on behaving differently in class for the rest of the week. The following note was given to Ms. Lee.

Dear Ms. Lee,

Thank you for your referral of Don G. We have met and he has told me his plans for acting slightly different in your class for the rest of the week. Please notice any differences in your class that work better for Don and jot them down. We will appreciate your observations!

Thanks!

LM and Don

Alternative school or bust: A case study

I once worked with Josh, an eighth-grade boy who was, in his words, "on my way to alternative school". The student was not at all worried about his future transfer, for he had heard it would be less work and much quieter. As we talked, his arms were crossed tightly across his chest and his attitude was that of pride/anger/rebellion/resistance, all rolled up into one! Diverting for a moment from the issue of alternative school, he mentioned how his father drank heavily and often had severe arguments with him in which he called him names and criticized him for everything. With this information in mind, I inquired about how he was still able to go to school with all of that happening at home. I chose to be quiet for a while during our time and align closely with his world view. At the end of the session, I asked if he might be willing to stay out of alternative school for one more week, since he obviously needed to show some people that he could do whatever he put his mind to. He agreed that there indeed were some people (Dad) who needed to see him differently. I then asked him, "What do you hope they will soon see in you that will tell them they are wrong about you?" He replied that he wanted people to see that he was really a good kid who just wanted to be left alone. (He had been bothered by gangs.) I agreed with him and told him I suspected that staying out of alternative school for another week would probably do that. He agreed. He stayed out of alternative school permanently. His teachers reported to his mother that they had seen a vast improvement in his interest at school and his behavior. I'm still not certain what occurred in our meeting that caused such a change in Josh ... nor does it matter.

Today's teachers and counselors struggle with students who refuse to take responsibility for their actions and are resistant to authority and compliance. This age-old struggle is simply a trait of childhood and adolescence, yet educators (and the world) appropriately perceive self-evaluation, responsibility, and change in behaviors as necessary for growth. A normal response to resistance is to be resistant. However, this merry-go-round of interactions rarely works. Like two boxers moving towards each other with their fists up, neither allows the other the first punch. Resistant teachers and students are the same. The ideas of intervening with *competency-based conversations* as introduced in Chapter Three tend to lessen resistance and open up possibilities without blaming. Nonetheless, methods tried in various educational settings have seemed to focus around evaluative methods that diagnose and label students and their behaviors instead of noting times when the negative behaviors are nonexistent. As previous chapters have pointed out, this information holds little value for current strategies or solutions.

Too often, however, students see their efforts at solving problems as defective and tend to give up all hope. They tend to blame the parents or teachers and sit back waiting for *them* to change. Waiting can cost grades, reputations, and self esteem. The Student Information Sheet given here grew from students' suggestions that their teachers simply did not know what helped them in class. Often it is the perception of being bad, blamed, not liked, not understood, and not listened to that enables poor communication and stifles cooperation from students. The counselor can offer the student an opportunity to "tell us what we need to know about you, you are the expert!"

The Student Information Sheet (Metcalf, 1995, p. 129) is a different exercise for most students (and parents and teachers) and can be even more effective when done collaboratively with an administrator or parent. The counselor/administrator phrases the purpose as such:

"You know, I truly believe that we just simply do not understand what you need from us here at Smith Junior High School. You have done well during the past six months, but obviously things are changing for you that we don't have information for. Today, I'd like you to do an inventory for us, and watch as you go through your day for times when you do okay in class."

As the student watches her behavior, the probability is that she will change behaviors as well. Asking the student to talk to teachers about her needs will increase collaboration between teacher and student as well. A shy student may prefer placing the form in her teacher's box or give it directly to the teacher. The importance of this venture is to let the teacher know that the student is attempting to change. With high school students, this form may not be necessary, but the idea is still helpful. A conference with a high school teacher might offer the student an opportunity to tell her what she needs from the teacher. Preparing the teacher beforehand about how the student will approach the conference might be valuable. Often, one-on-one with teachers is difficult for students. The teacher could be informed that the student wants to try a different approach to working things out; instead of talking about the problem, the teacher wants to discuss what might be helpful to the student's learning, behaving, or participating in class.

In addition, this exercise teaches students to *look at themselves differently*, as if they are able to accomplish tasks. The students have a better chance to become the expert on themselves and are more likely to ask themselves a question—such as "What works for me?"—*the next time they experience a problem*. If we, as educators, can assist school clients with this practical way of perceiving and dealing with life, we have truly given them a gift for a less-stressful life.

The parent conference: an opportunity for requesting parental cooperation

The Parent Conference Role Play included here shows how the Student Information Sheet, the Teacher Information for Students sheet, and parent conference dialogue can collaboratively work to discover solutions that work for all involved (Metcalf, 1995, p. 133). The dialogue represents efforts on the part of all concerned and creates the atmosphere of responsibility on the part of everyone to stop maintaining "the problem".

Student Information Sheet

Name of Student: _____ Date: _____

Dear Student,

Your teachers and I are interested in assisting you here at school. Below, please list the times when you think you do *better* in school. (Think about the past few months or last year.) Be specific. This is your chance to tell us what you think will help you do better more often.

For example, "I do better in school when I think the teacher likes me … I understand the homework assignment … I place my assignment in my book to turn it in … when the teacher calls on me … when the teacher does not ignore my answer, etc."

1. _____

2. _____

3. _____

4. _____

5. _____

What worked for me in class this week:

_____

_____

_____

_____

_____

_____

_____

_____

_____

_____

Student Signature

For many parents, a conference entails hearing about how bad things are at school, and many parents consider themselves failures, or feel that the school has failed their child. The dialogue given in the reproducible represents how solution-focused brief therapy can rescue the school, teachers, and administrators from being blamed. The dialogue spreads the responsibility throughout the system involved—everyone's ideas are solicited and considered before the strategy is developed.

As the language suggests, the school, parent, and student agree that success lies in the solutions noticed by all involved. Notice the language used in the dialogue: *"when _____ does better"*, *"what will you get to do when _____ does better?"* This suggestion that things will improve encourages hope. Parents who have children in trouble at school often come to school concerned and feeling like failures. By offering suggestions of the teachers, students, and parents themselves, there is virtually no threat of failure. I tend to mention in training sessions that I never ask anyone to do anything that they have never done before. There is no risk of failure that way. Instead, I may suggest they do more of what worked in other situations. A mom who worries about her 16-year-old daughter's association with friends she does not know can observe how she has set limits with her driving last summer. The daughter always told her where she was going and with whom when she drove the car or she lost the privilege for a day. By applying the same ideas for friends by requiring her daughter to introduce her friends, leave a phone number or address as to her destination—or she loses a night out—the mom may worry less and feel more comfortable.

Concluding comments

The school program described in Chapter Four developed from a belief that ideas are helpful when they adapt and change according to the needs of your students, who will inevitably teach you about themselves if you allow them to. The chapter invites you to put aside assumptions that problems are too difficult to solve when the student does not seem to be motivated to change. There are 20 or 30 minds placed in seats every day in your classroom. Give one of them a day to remember tomorrow.

Parent Conference Role Play

The following statements and questions are suggestions that might be useful in making parent conferences more pleasant and empowering to students and their parents.

1. Information Gathering–Parent Empowerment

"Mrs. _____, I want you to know how impressed I am that you came so easily (willingly) to our meeting. Obviously you know that _____ needs your assistance."

"Can you tell me exactly what you're seeing at home or at school regarding _____ that concerns you?"

"You know, that's really in agreement with what we're seeing in _____ here at (school)."

2. Searching for Exceptions

"Mrs. _____, I'm, really curious about the times when you do not see _____ experiencing troubles with his/her schoolwork. Can you tell me about those times (even if you need to go back a month/or year(s))?"

"What days, how many hours a week, times a week, do you notice _____ not experiencing troubles?"

'So, when _____ is (on a schedule, when you're right there with him/her, when you check his/her work, when he/she is not fighting with siblings, when his/her homework is done on time, when he/she thinks the teacher likes him/her, etc.), school is a little easier, is that correct?"

3. Changing from Problem Thinking to Solution Thinking

"That's really interesting, Mrs. _____, because when I asked the teacher(s) who referred _____ to me to fill out the sheets I have here (Teacher Referral Forms) I found there were similar times to what you're describing, plus other times when _____ did better. These sheets, Mrs. _____, list the times here at (school) when _____ does better in class. We're interested in those times here because we really want _____ to succeed."

"I have one more sheet to share with you, Mrs. _____. It's a sheet that your child filled out for us. On this sheet, again, are _____'s views about when school goes better for him/her. She/he said that he/she does better in class when (she feels the teacher likes her, she is not so tired, when she is not sitting in the back of the room, when she is not worried about you and her dad, when she spends time with you, when she does not have to babysit during week nights, etc.)."

4. Developing Tasks for Solutions

"Mrs. _____, based on what _____ has told us works for him/her, and what his/her teachers have said works better and what you have said works, what would you suggest we try with _____ for a few days this week?"

5. Suggesting Success

"Mrs. _____, I appreciate your time today. Your suggestions really make sense. I guess I'd like to ask you one more quick question:

"When _____ does better more often in school and you see that happening, what will you and _____ get to do more of that you aren't doing now?"

Chapter Four Practice Exercise

Defeating School Problems

With the following tools at your fingertips (plus many of your own!), respond differently this week to one student who has been perplexing to you. You will need:

- Teacher Referral Form

- Student Information Sheet

- Scaling Questions

Talk to your colleagues and invite them to observe the student and look for exceptions instead of problems. Send a note home to the student's parents with exceptions written from the past week. Ask the parents to also observe their child or adolescent at home for other times when he or she cooperates well, studies better, or responds to directions more efficiently. Consider parents another set of eyes to help you be more competent with the student in the classroom. This assignment will take about 30 minutes to do. It will be worth it when your classroom runs more smoothly and your student reacts differently toward you.

Something Exciting Has Happened at School

Dear Parent,

I have been watching _____ this week and have noticed the following fine qualities about _____:

1. _____

   _____

2. _____

   _____

_____

Teacher Signature

Chapter Five
Working with the Academically Challenged Student

"Whether you think you can or you can't, you're right."

—Henry Ford

The student in the back row is two years behind in reading. You have tried referring him to the reading specialist, but her program is full. When you suggested that the school counselor test him for special education, his test scores came back too high. You also talked to his parents who said you had to find a way to teach their son. "I am a classroom teacher, not a special education teacher, I don't have the extra time to work just with him. I have twenty-six other students!" Your justification is real and your complaint is valid. Besides, you have not been trained to do remedial reading work. Yet the student remains in your classroom. When he is not kept busy, he is misbehaving. He often wanders around disturbing other students. Perhaps he has even been told that he can't learn well so he doesn't try to learn in the first place, as the first case study will reveal. Yet your job is to teach him. You are expected to help him progress and sometimes your competency and evaluations depend on his success. It doesn't seem fair. This is the reality of today's classroom teacher and the academically challenged student.

Desperately seeking the yellow brick road

We live in a world where people assume they must refer people to help them. There is always someone brighter, smarter, more experienced, more skillful, and more educated to whom we look as having the answer. While we do this with good intentions, the referred person begins to think that there *is* something *wrong with him* and we begin to believe that we can't be helpful. Yet sooner or later, those referred must stop and be helped, *if* there is room and *if* there is funding to support it. Larry Furmancyzk, a school counselor and therapist in Prince George, British Columbia once commented to me on this dilemma:

> It seems that we have all become Dorothy's, pointing towards the yellow brick road as the only road to solutions for students. Because there exists this idea that a yellow brick road exists, we cease trying and refer. We seem to think that referring is the only way to resolve a learning or behavioral problem. Yet, when the student reaches the Wizard, he meets someone who does not have all the answers, and, in fact, is too removed from the student's situation to know how to help her completely. Somehow, we have to create enough confidence in ourselves as teachers, counselors, and parents to help the student ourselves.

We have to stop referring students unless it is absolutely necessary. Students have abilities in other areas, we have to discover what works in those areas and put those strategies to work in the classroom. More than anything, in order to help them believe in themselves as competent, we have to believe that we are competent too.

Henry Levin, a Stanford University economist and educator, for the past decade has been against categorizing students. He thinks more commitment on the part of teachers to find a way to reach a student will take us where we want to go ... towards academic excellence. "Anytime you start to sort out kids, you eventually build categories with given assumptions," Levin says, "If you start off saying this child is at risk, you're saying this child is defective. So we send the child to the repair shop. The problem is, you'll never make the child whole when you stigmatize the child in every possible way. You make the child see that he or she isn't as good as the others. And in the meantime, other kids are moving ahead. Once the child is in the repair shop, he or she will never be out of the repair shop" (Levin, 1994, p. 47). In Levin's "accelerated school", textbooks have been replaced by magazines, newspapers, and a wide variety of books that appeal to all learners. Parents roam the halls between their volunteer shifts and rows of desks are abandoned in favor of a cooperative learning approach. Students gather in groups, and teachers and aides circulate around the classrooms. All students are expected to reach the goals set by the school and the school pushes the students in a variety of ways so that students reach the expectations.

The multi-learning styles classroom has arrived

If you are a classroom teacher, sooner or later you will be faced with the challenge of having one student—or several students—in your classroom who learn differently and require a multitude of skills and time to help them to succeed. Perhaps it will happen when the principal refuses your referral to special education because the student's parents refuse to admit that the student has special needs. Maybe it will be the school counselor whose test scores reveal that the student is capable of learning and doesn't qualify for special programs. Or maybe it is the special education student who is included in

A Personal Inventory: What Do You Do When the Mission Seems Impossible?

Think about the following questions as they relate to how you deal with challenging, seemingly impossible situations in your personal and professional life. Think about the ways you take on challenges with your own children, your relatives, spouse, or significant other. Reminisce about earlier days when you were younger and able to tackle even the most difficult situations. Consider your strengths and abilities with your colleagues and best friends and search for what works for you when life seems impossible to change.

1. When you are faced with a personal dilemma that seems impossible to solve or com plete within a certain amount of time, what do you do? List at least three strategies below.

   a._____

   b. _____

   c._____

2. How would you explain the way you are thinking about the problem as you persevere to finish the task to solve it?

   a._____

   b. _____

   c._____

3. What effective personal skills do you use in social situations or at home with your family or significant other that are helpful during those challenging, problem-ridden situations?

   a._____

   b. _____

   c._____

4. Think of the last time a problem affected a friend, colleague, or relative who was very important to you. How did you assist them in dealing with their struggle? What steps did you specifically take that seemed to help them? How did you keep yourself on track during the situation instead of giving up?

   a._____

   b. _____

   c._____

5. When you begin using some of the ideas that you have described in 1, 2, 3 and 4 during the next week with a challenging student in your classroom, what will you see yourself doing that will be slightly helpful to the student?

   a._____

   b. _____

   c._____

your class so that she may experience a regular classroom, yet can't seem to understand the lessons. Today we face the challenge of helping those who learn differently and are asked to be an expert on teaching them the basics. Believing that we can each be experts in helping our challenging students ever so slightly is our first step to making a difference in their lives. To adopt this difficult new belief, it is helpful to reflect on how you deal with the other stressful, challenging situations in your life that can seem impossible to solve. The inventory given here can assist you in discovering your personal strategies during such events.

Finding the expert teacher within

What did you discover about your inner strengths and values that assist you daily in coping with your personal life? Chances are you never thought of how you sequentially dealt with very important challenges or problems. These are the same strategies to consider when you are faced with a challenging student and are feeling powerless to help him or her. There are probably students in your classes with the following impossible scenarios:

- no family support
- no social skills
- poor reading scores
- attention problems
- poor verbal skills
- lack of confidence

Looking at how the lives of our students are *always* affected by our actions, it makes sense to dig deep into our pockets for our personal skills and believe in ourselves enough to do something different for students who are experiencing the troubles listed. In Chapter Five, many ideas will be shared to encourage and give you confidence that you *can* reach and teach the academically challenged student who remains in your classroom after your attempt to refer her fails. Sometimes the methods that unfold will be quite novel and new to you. You may find, for example, that the ADHD student will complete his spelling words if he stands rather than sits. You may discover that the junior high girl who talks excessively does her reading best when allowed to sit outside the classroom away from her friends. You may find that the 18-year-old disadvantaged male will be more prone to read if the book is the driver's license manual. The fifth-grade boy may begin to finish his math when he is allowed to add and subtract *in his head* rather than on paper. Whatever the solution, you may find that when you meet resistance in the classroom, it's time to cooperate with where the student is. In other words, it's time to stop trying to change students to *fit your* description and believe in who the student is and help him or her tell you what would work instead.

Solution-focused skills, ideas, and suggestions for thinking about the academically challenging student will be provided so that you may brainstorm with parents and colleagues while writing a new Solution-Focused Individual Education Plan for the academically challenged student. The first case presented here will serve as an example of what this chapter endorses. Whether you are an elementary or a secondary teacher, special education teacher, or alternative education teacher, notice what happens when your definition of success challenges your student's definition of success. Realize that you can begin tomorrow in your own classroom with a new perception and an intention to change the student's reality.

Will it be Metallica or Mozart with your English lesson?

By Ms. Toy Angell, Teacher

Mark was a student in my tenth-grade class who was labeled as a special education student. When I first met Mark, he was listening to Metallica on his headphones during

class. He would constantly interrupt my class with a question of "Miss, I don't know what you mean", and various other remarks made with a child-like voice. During the first two weeks of the semester I talked to Mark whenever I could about anything. One day after a review for an upcoming achievement test, I asked Mark if he had completed the class questions. Mark replied:

"No, I'm a Special Ed student so I can't do it anyway."

I then asked him who had told him that he couldn't do something. He said:

"It's obvious that I can't. They (the staff) don't make me take the test because they know I couldn't pass it. Besides, my parents have always told me I was stupid."

I was taken back by Mark's reply. After the class was over I stressed with him that he should never hide behind a label because it keeps the individual named Mark from doing whatever he put his mind to. He had a hard time listening, however, since the headphones were still too loud. I asked him why he wore the headphones and he told me "to keep the noise out and focus". I became very interested in him at that moment and asked him what he was listening to. He showed me a variety of hard rock CDs. I told him about an interesting study done with Mozart and classical music and learning. I asked him if he wouldn't mind trying that kind of music and that we could do our own study to see if it would help him to learn. While he never picked up the Mozart CD I brought to class, his taste in music did change to a more (quiet) type. Within a week he stopped bringing the earphones to class!

He began to direct his attention to me through class questions and between conversations as he left the class each day. One day I graded essays. I had each student talk to me outside in the hallway for privacy. As I talked to Mark, I noticed that he would not look at me when I talked to him about his essay. I stopped talking and would only talk to him when he looked me in the eyes. He looked at me quite puzzled. I explained to him the significance of looking into someone's eyes and focusing on what they say. Somehow the conversation was directed to his Special Ed label. He said that when he was little his parents bragged on his big vocabulary but something happened and their interest in him stopped. Soon everyone began telling him that he was stupid. I asked him:

"How do you think I see you?"

He told me:

"You're different. You think I can do anything I want to. You think I'm nice."

I told him that he was correct and then I asked him who he thought knew more about this subject, everyone or me. He said that I did and he smiled. I told him that if anyone says he can't do something that it should make him happy because they have just dared him to succeed and I knew he was the kind of guy who enjoys doing better than expected. He sat up straight and said "okay". Before he went back to class I assured him that I would probably hear of a guy inventing something really cool one day and his name would be Mark. If I was lucky, he would remember his tenth-grade English teacher.

When I began the King Arthur section in English the next week, I required the students to keep up with many papers. Mark was no exception. When he missed a class or fell behind, I simply told him that I would see him either at tutoring or at lunch and it was his choice, but he *had* to do the work. He started making regular visits by the class and during transition periods. I would always greet him and ask how he was that day. If he walked by the door and I waved, he waved back. Together we overcame his fear of talking in front of the class so he could present his paper. He did very well. He found me on the last day of school in the teacher's lounge. He told me that he wanted to get me a card but he couldn't afford it. He handed me a note which I read and made me cry. I hugged him and told him that I didn't doubt that he would be a success. This is what the note said:

Ms. Angell, you have been a very wonderful teacher and have gone beyond the limit for me you've taught me so much about myself and King Arthur no teacher or person for that matter has ever given me the Inspiration to work Hard for something and to reach a goal and in return all I can do is thank you for everything and wish you the best of Luck and I could only wish every teacher was like you cause there's not enough teachers like you.

Good bye I'll miss you

Mark

Changing descriptions can change the outcome

What happened when Ms. Angell heard Mark's description of himself? She didn't adopt his description because she figured that it was trapping him into believing that he couldn't perform. If she agreed with it she would have guaranteed more of the same. If she disagreed with it as his teacher, she would send him a different message. When people perceive themselves a certain way, they behave as such. Old beliefs can be roadblocks to motivation and learning new concepts. Praise alone is not enough. When a teacher praises a student who feels badly about himself, the student often does not believe the compliment. When a teacher asks a student, "How were you able to be successful at that moment?" the student becomes an expert on an event that the teacher is questioning about. The teacher is no longer the expert, describing to the student what he or she did well, but an onlooker who notices a success that the student had overlooked. This interaction is quite powerful in helping students to look at themselves differently.

Creating new descriptions

Here are some points adapted from the work of Bill O'Hanlon (1996) to think about while attempting to change students' descriptions of themselves so that they become more productive. Sometimes all it takes is a new definition of oneself to push a little harder. As you read the ideas, think of a particular student who has you concerned about his or her academic success.

1. **Find out about other people who do not view the student as incapable.**
   Ask the student: *"Who in your life sees you when you are doing things well?"*

   Ask colleagues: *"Who has noticed when _____ is slightly successful?"*

129

2. **Find out about hidden or unnoticeable aspects of the student or the student's life that are different and more successful than the unsuccessful times. Ask the student to explain what goes on during the more successful times.**
   Ask the student: *"When is it that life works for you and you feel slightly better about yourself?"*

   Ask colleagues: *"What's unique about _____?"*

3. **Find out about the student's best moments ... the times when he or she thinks good things about himself or herself.**
   Ask the student: *"Tell me about something that people don't always see in you."*

   Ask colleagues: *"When have you noticed _____ feeling slightly more confident?"*

4. **Connect the student with other students who once felt slightly down about themselves but found a way out.**
   Say to student: *"I would like you to sit with Joey. Joey has recently found a way to finish his spelling words in twenty minutes."*

   Ask colleagues: *"In what situation have you noticed _____ working well with others?"*

5. **Normalize the student by letting her know that others have experienced difficulties similar to hers. If possible, self disclose that you once had something similar happen to you.**
   Say to student: *"I really understand how tough things are. I recall a student I had last year whose grandmother passed away. She learned that after a week or two she felt a little better when she took a minute a day to think really special thoughts about her grandmother. Is there something special about her that you would like to tell me?"*

6. **Ask the student to experiment with different ways of being in the same situation rather than stay stuck in the same pattern that does not work.**
   Ask the student: *"I wonder what small experiment we could do this morning while you work on your math problems so that you finish them quickly? Let's come up with a plan! You start."*

This desk is not off limits!

How do your students view you? Would they say that you are accessible or that your desk is off limits? Our presence in the classroom creates the mood for learning. We have the power when we walk in the room to motivate or destroy a student's desire to learn. This is a huge responsibility! We take risks each time we talk to a student or a parent,

design a lesson plan, or order a new textbook. Our discussions, compliments, comments, and opinions are important to our students even when they don't admit it. I talked once with a high school junior, age 17, about his school performance. His parents were very concerned about his school performance since he wanted to graduate with his class—but out of the six classes he was taking, he was failing two of them. He said he knew he was not doing the work as he needed to, but he felt he was too far behind to catch up on his assignments, so he basically just quit. He was a likable student who was constantly pursued to do all types of computer graphics and video taping for many faculty members and board members. He bragged to me that he had never missed a day of high school. He liked school and enjoyed seeing his friends. He just could not seem to get it together to pass all of his classes.

As we talked, I asked him what the four teachers out of six did that helped him to pass their classes and keep him motivated to keep trying and turning in his work. I also asked him to think of how other teachers in the past had assisted him to be successful since he had obviously made it to eleventh grade. After a few minutes of thought, he admitted that school had always been a struggle and that he had barely made it to the next grade each year. Then he said the following thoughtful statements:

"Some of them really pushed me in the classroom and that worked for me. I get too distracted and sometimes leave without turning in the work that I do. I do my homework and forget to turn it in all the time. I have an attention problem and a vision problem that I've had since elementary school and it's too hard for me to remember everything that I'm supposed to do. It's not an excuse, it's just what happens. Last year my History teacher always reminded me to turn in my definitions before I left her class. After a while I remembered myself because it became a habit."

"I like worksheets and fill-in-the-blank–type papers because they help me to focus on what's important in the book. Reading and concentrating is hard so when I have a sheet to tell me what answers are important, I understand what to study for the test. I do really bad on questions that take lots of thought. I do much better when the answer is just straightforward. In my Sociology class this year my teacher did that . . . she even let us use the worksheets on tests. She made out the tests so that the answers weren't on the worksheets, they just helped us think of the right answers."

"I've had about twenty teachers in the past three years. Out of the twenty, about two of my teachers didn't care if I asked them for help but the others just didn't want you near their desk, like it was irritating to them that you were even there. If I didn't feel comfortable talking to those teachers, I didn't. Those who I couldn't talk to always gave me consequences, too. That never worked for me. Either I want to do the work or I don't. Those teachers who seemed to like me and take the time taught the classes I always passed because I told them what I needed and they always listened."

131

There are many students whose view of themselves is so poor that they perform way below their abilities. Imagine if most of those students became motivated just because you told them *in a different way* that they were so important to you that you were willing to do anything to help them succeed. Imagine if they suddenly saw your desk as accessible and that you were willing to take the first step and ask, "What have other teachers done before that helped you to perform better?" The solution-focused teacher does what works and doesn't repeat what did not work in the past. The teacher is approachable because he or she respects the student's needs and seeks out those needs when the student doesn't offer to explain them. Although the solution-focused teacher is busy like everyone else, this teacher realizes that asking a student what he needs from him or her takes less than 15 seconds out of a day consisting of 8 hours. The solution-focused teacher knows that discovering what will work for a student will not only help the student but it will help the teacher's class management, lesson planning, and class morale.

Going the extra mile like this is difficult and sometimes uncomfortable because it means that the teacher must give up on pushing his goal onto his student and listen for what the student needs. Interestingly enough, often the student's goal will match the teacher's:

Teacher: You seem down today. What's going on?

Student: My old man is on me about my Algebra grade.

Teacher: That's too bad. What would it take for him to get off your back about it?

Student: Pass, of course.

Teacher: You are five points from passing, do you realize that?

Student: I'm failing and if I don't bring up the grade I have to quit football.

Teacher: You're five points away from passing. What do you think you and I could do to gain five points so your dad gives you a break and you can keep playing?

Student: It's the homework. I do it but I forget to turn it in. Sometimes it's too hard and I just give up, too.

Teacher: Has that ever happened in any other classes and then you fixed it?

Student: I used to go in to my History class last semester during homeroom period and finish my definitions. My teacher gave me a pass.

Teacher: When do you think you could come in here each day?

Student: Probably after last period because I have thirty minutes before football practice.

The teacher's past experiences have taught her that the goal and strategies surrounding the work would result in a positive outcome if only the student would try it. However, if it is the teacher's goal and not the student's, the efforts are prone to failure. It is better to help the student develop his or her own goal, as the student did here. When students feel that their teacher is committed to their learning, they become more committed as well. Don't forget to follow up with the student the next day and ask what went a little better for him or her. If the student does not know, compliment him or her on something, even if it is as simple as "I am still impressed that you want things to be better and are so willing to make this effort."

Succeeding at reading without the wizard's help

This chapter has suggested that digging deeper into academic issues is not always necessary in order to be helpful to students. However, sometimes colleagues and parents insist on digging deeper into the academic problem in an attempt to identify problems instead of focusing on solutions. In this case, the respectful stance to take is that of acknowledging their needs and helping them explore *how understanding will aid them in planning*. This means asking  the parents or colleague how it will be helpful to know the composition of the problem and then leading them into a discussion of a student's abilities instead of deficits. When the teacher hears the answer, the answer can become part of the goal-setting procedure. The following case study follows this strategy and shows how a teacher can take specific steps to involve the student, parents, and herself collaboratively to fight the problem and achieve success.

Susan

Ten-year-old Susan was having difficulties in reading. The school counselor wanted to steer the parents and classroom teacher past the problems and help them to identify Susan's resources and abilities. Her parents and teacher had requested testing early in the school year and test scores simply revealed a learning difference in reading, keeping her behind her peers. Susan's progress was slow during the year and her parents began looking for more testing, believing that there could be better instruction when they understood more about why their child couldn't read well. Her teacher was upset that she was not at grade level and her parents were upset that she wouldn't read on her own. Her mother had attempted to get Susan to read by herself at home, particularly during the summer months, but she refused. The parents continued to look to everyone else in the school to solve the problem, since they felt helpless. They did not know what to do next. Instead of referring Susan for tutoring in reading, the school counselor was determined to keep Susan in her regular classroom.

The following steps make up The S.M.A.R.T. Program I developed for teachers to use when working with students like Susan (Metcalf, 1997, p. 163).

The S.M.A.R.T. Program (Solutions for Motivation and Academic Resources in Teaching)

Step One: Identifying the Goal and the Customer

The customer is the person(s) requesting help. In this case the customers were the teacher and Susan's parents. The goal of Susan's parents and teacher was to help Susan progress in her reading ability. They knew that she would be successful when she progressed closer to her grade level in reading. This was a goal that could be measured. It was very important to hear everyone's goal for the student. The teacher would have to enlist Susan as a customer later. For now, those who were the most concerned had some homework to do of their own. It would be important later to collaborate with the academically challenged student so that everyone in the "system" moved in the same direction. To enlist the cooperation of everyone, the teacher listened to the concerns of the parents respectfully when she placed the first phone call to them. After hearing their worries, she found it helpful to offer them the following scale while identifying their goal for their daughter. Using the scale keeps the expectations realistic and helps everyone involved to see the progress as something that happens one step at a time:

Say: *"On a scale of 1–10, with a '10' meaning she has reached grade level and a '1' meaning that she can't read at all, where is she at this time?"*

can't read _____ reads at grade level

       1   2   3   4   5   6   7   8   9   10

At the end of the phone conversation, Susan's teacher told her parents that she would be sending them an observation sheet (Parent Observation of Academic Success) to fill out before their first meeting at school. The teacher also told them that she was going to talk to Susan and do some observations of Susan's school success on her own (Teacher Observation of Academic Success). She made a point to emphasize the need for everyone to focus on *what works* with Susan rather than what is not working.

Step Two: Looking for Exceptions to the Problem

The teacher observed the times when Susan performed adequately in school, particularly in activities involving reading which were surprising. She then learned the following exceptions about Susan's school work and home life surrounding school that gave her hope and ideas for the meeting with her parents:

1. Susan often raises her hand to read aloud in the classroom.

2. Susan is quite distractible, so the medication that she takes works to help her focus.

3. When Susan's assignments are modified and shorter, she feels less overwhelmed and completes them.

4. Susan had achieved a grade level of reading through past instruction, even though she was behind. This told me she was capable of learning some reading skills.

5. Susan does better with more attention from the teacher. It keeps her focused and on track.

6. Susan performs at grade level in math and enjoys doing math assignments on the class computer.

7. Since the beginning of the school year, Susan has improved her reading slightly.

The teacher composed a list of these exceptions by using the Teacher Observation of Academic Success sheet and made copies for everyone involved. She then asked Susan's parents to go over their Parent Observation of Academic Success and made a copy. The next reproducible, Solving School Problems *with* Students, was designed to help teachers talk with students of all ages about their school life. Susan's teacher spoke with Susan before the meeting with her parents. The words can be changed to accommodate specific ages, but the steps should remain the same. The resulting answers will prove to be invaluable as the teacher and parents collaborate on ways to help the student *according to the student*.

Step Three: Suggesting Competency to the Student's Current System
The student's *current system* refers to those involved in her academic success. In Susan's case, the system consisted of her parents, teacher(s), and school counselor. When the parents met with the teacher, the following dialogue was suggested:

"Suppose we thought about this situation slightly differently. Suppose there were no other programs for Susan to attend and no more tests to give her. Suppose the task to assist Susan in becoming as successful as she can be depended only on us. Based on the ideas on the list here, let's brainstorm some strategies for Susan as we go over each of these exceptions."

Parent Observation of Academic Success

Name of Student _____ Date _____

Teacher _____ Class/Grade _____

On the lines below, please recall the grade level(s) in which your child/adolescent has been successful over the past few years. What teaching methods seemed to work best for your child/adolescent?

_____

_____

_____

When your child/adolescent struggles with certain subjects or classes, what strategies do you sometimes use to assist him/her that work? What do you do at home when your child/adolescent is upset or disillusioned about a situation or project?

_____

_____

_____

List the type of teacher who seems to reach and teach your child/adolescent best. What does the teacher specifically do that makes the difference in keeping your child interested and focused on doing his/her best?

_____

_____

_____

What has your child/adolescent's teacher done this year that has been effective?

_____

_____

_____

What have you done to help your child/adolescent this year that has been effective and helpful?

_____

_____

_____

Teacher Observation of Academic Success

Name of Student _____ Date _____

Subject/Class _____ Teacher _____

Below, list activities in which the student was able to achieve at least partial success. Mention what the student did to be successful and the teaching method used. Rate the student's progress on a scale of 1–10 with 1 = not successful and 10 = completely successful.

Activity/Assignment: _____

Performance: _____

Teaching Method: _____

Rating: _____

Activity/Assignment: _____

Performance: _____

Teaching Method: _____

Rating: _____

Activity/Assignment: _____

Performance: _____

Teaching Method: _____

Rating: _____

Solving School Problems *with* Students

A Brainstorming Sheet for Teachers to Use with Students

1. Get the student's view of the problem and define a goal with her. Say:
   "Susie, this seems tough for you right now. How do you want things to be for your-self in school?"

   _____

   _____

   "If I gave you a scale of 1–10, where a '10' meant that things were going perfectly for you in school and a '1' meant that things were going very poorly, where would you place yourself at this time?"

   _____

   "What would I see you doing just for this afternoon (elementary) or week (secondary) that would help you to move up just one small step on that scale? What specifically would that look like?"

   _____

   _____

   If the student tells you what someone else would be doing, agree with her and then say: 'I know, but we can't change him. What can you do so that things are better for *you*?"

   _____

   _____

2. Search for problem-free times with the student. Say:
   "Susie, can you take me back to a time when this problem did not bother you and you passed … (subject)?"

   "What did you do then that helped you to be more successful? How did you manage to do that?"

   _____

   _____

   "Tell me what other teachers have done before that was really helpful to you?" (Ask this several times so that you have many exceptions.)

   _____

   _____

3. As her teacher, add your own observations of when school works for her. (See the Teacher Observation of Academic Success sheet.) Ask the student if the observations that you made are correct.

A Brainstorming Sheet for Teachers to Use with Students *(continued)*

"I noticed that when I told everyone to turn in their spelling words yesterday, you were able to put them in the green box on my desk. Does it help for me to remind you? I will if you want me to."

_____

_____

Ask the student what else you have done at other times that helped the problem to be smaller.

_____

_____

"I notice that you like looking at picture books almost more than the word books. Tell me, what is it about the picture books that you like so much?" (An exception)

_____

_____

4. Inquire about how parents or significant others can assist the student.

   "Suppose you woke up tomorrow morning and a miracle had taken place. Not only was school going well for you, but at home, your parents were doing things that also helped you to be successful in school. What would they be doing differently?"

   _____

   _____

   "Is it okay that I tell your parents your ideas when I meet with them?"
   _____ yes _____ no

5. Compliment the student on any efforts that you have seen her take to work through the school problem. Then ask:

   "What do you think you should keep on doing that is working for you at this point?"

   _____

   _____

   "What can I do to help?"

   _____

   _____

Observations of Parents (review of Parent Observations of Academic Success form)

"Let's look at how Susan has learned best in the past and stayed on task. If you would, review with me the observations you made on the sheet I gave to you. (Make copies.) Suppose we developed a few strategies for helping Susan at home, based on what you have found has worked for her in school. Mom and Dad, what would you begin to suggest doing with Susan at home on a very small scale, based on your observations?"

"Tell me about the times when you succeed in getting Susan to do something at home when she did not want to do it. How did you get her to cooperate?"

"I wonder how your techniques there might translate into helping her 'practice' reading at home?"

"I notice, too, that Susan volunteers to read in class. It sounds like reading aloud to you at home might work. What do you think? Where/when would you suggest that she do that, just on a small scale, to help her to practice her reading?" (This will give parents more responsibility to choose and implement helpful strategies.)

Observations from the Teacher (review Teacher Observation of Academic Success form)

"Sounds like more attention works for Susan. I am going to give you a copy of some observations I made last week. (Make copies.) It also sounds like shorter assignments are more easily completed. I've located some computer software to help Susan to work on her reading since she enjoys the computer so much. Whenever there is an assignment that Susan finds too difficult, I will put her at the computer to complete a modified assignment. She works well with groups. There is a buddy system where older children read to the kindergarten class. I have submitted Susan's name. She will begin reading aloud to them on Thursday."

In addition, it helps to expand the system sometimes to gather more potential exceptions. I suggested that another teacher, school counselor, parent, or the school psychologist sit in the classroom for a day or two, fill out an additional Teacher Observation of Academic Success sheet and notice when Susan stays on task and is more attentive and productive. After a period of two weeks (or whenever the system decides), Susan and her parents met again to scale Susan's progress. Upon resumption of the meeting, I encouraged the teacher to begin the meeting with: "Let's talk about what's going better for Susan." The second meeting can then end with a compilation of information from parents, teacher, and student, developing a Solution-Focused Individual Education Plan (IEP) as follows.

The development of the Solution-Focused IEP grew from my personal experience with such meetings. My youngest son's short attention span was affecting his learning and efficiency in class and, together, his teachers and I wanted to do something different for him. After sitting through the meeting with his vice principal, speech therapist, and three of his teachers, I wondered, "Where do we go now?" I curiously asked the two teachers what they thought they did that helped him remember to turn in his assignments and bring home his homework. As they described what they thought they did, his third teacher acknowledged that she might try their tactics as well. I felt very fortunate to have worked with such a receptive staff. The ideas were readily accepted and implemented. He began to do much better in class.

What can I do when the parents are not interested in helping?

When parents do not have the time or want to take the time to come to school and offer assistance, do what *they* are not doing for their child/adolescent ... be there. Use the Teacher Observation for Academic Success and give copies to other teachers who have contact with the student. Get the principal or vice principal to fill out a copy. Then have your own team meeting with the student and discuss what the student feels is helpful and share your observations. In other words, create a support system that says "we are here to care for you". This sort of meeting is quite easily done with secondary students. They will appreciate you more than you will ever know. Elementary students will also appreciate 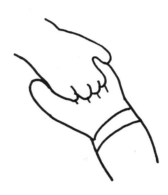 the meeting; however, they may need additional instructions as to how they will be helped on a daily basis. The "system" then comes alive for the student. Don't be surprised if the elementary student *clings* to you or those who are part of his system. You are giving the child an entity to which he can attach to ... finally. When this occurs, embrace the opportunity to give him something vital to his well being. As he *fills up* with your good intentions, he will back off and feel less needy. He finally will have someone in his corner who wants to take the time for him, and that is very attractive.

Vocational or academic programs? Designating the path

There will always be students whose IQ scores and abilities simply won't assist them in being scholars and there will always be teachers whose good intentions to make them scholars, fail. When this is the situation, the Brainstorming Toward Solutions worksheet is helpful for working toward solutions, or identifying alternative educational programs where the goal is to produce a functional, effective adult in society. You may find that persons using this sheet will want to steer backwards towards academics. If the student's test scores and school performance is *consistently* below average, gently prod those in the student's system with respectful questions and statements such as "Has that worked?" ... "That approach has not been helpful. Let's look at a alternative."

141

Concluding comments

The point of individual education plans should be to gather information that develops into a new and productive direction. Explanations of why students can't achieve are like barbed wired fences, only telling us what's wrong and what's not working. Exceptions tell us where to go and what works with student. In the same way that directions for a new gadget tell us how to assemble the parts, meetings for academically challenged students might need to include ideas that discuss what already works with a student, no matter how minimal his or her competencies may seem. This direction will assist teachers, administrators, and parents alike to focus on the student's competencies and their ability to help. It gives everyone in the student's system a feeling of goodwill and systemic collaboration.

The Solution-Focused Individual Education Plan (IEP)

Name of Student: _____ Date: _____ Grade: _____

A. Present Competencies

1. Physical, as it affects participation in instructional settings:

   _____ No physical limitations; no modification of regular class needed

   _____ Some physical limitations; no modification of regular class needed

   _____ Needs modifications because of the following impairment:

   _____

   *In what activities does the impairment *not* affect the student? List specific activities:

   _____

   _____

   *Describe modifications needed, based on the above activities:

   _____

   _____

2. Physical, as it affects physical education:
   _____ YES _____ NO The student is capable of receiving instruction in the essential elements of physical education through the regular program without modifications.

   *If NO, list the following activities in which the student has shown capabilities of receiving instruction: _____

   _____

   *Recommendation, based on competency in listed activities:

   _____

   _____

B. Behavioral

1. Educational placement and programming:

   _____ No modifications

   _____ Has some characteristics that may affect learning although not severe enough to withdraw from regular classes: _____ poor task completion: _____ impulsive—requires reminding to work slowly

   _____ Distractible—may require isolation, sit at front of room, etc., at times: _____

   other: _____

The Solution-Focused Individual Education Plan *(continued)*

*_____ Abilities that emerge in specific learning tasks/activities and enhance cooperation in the classroom, as identified by teachers, administrators, and parents:

_____

_____

_____

_____

2. Ability to follow disciplinary rules:

_____ Appropriate for age and cultural group. May be treated the same as non-handicapped student. Student should be able to follow the district's discipline management plan. Use of alternative educational placement and suspension as per TEA regulations is appropriate. Student is responsible for school board rules and campus policies without modifications.

*_____ This student is responsible for school board rules and campus procedure. A modified discipline plan will be utilized. The following approaches have been identified as effective in working with this student through direct observation by teachers, administrators, and parents:

_____

_____

_____

_____

C. Prevocational/Vocational (when appropriate): Skills that may be prerequisite to vocational education. Rate using the following scale: 1–10, where 1 = completely unskilled and 10 = completely competent:

_____	cognitive skills	_____	expressive skills
_____	reading level	_____	organizational skills
_____	performance	_____	social skills
_____	verbal comprehension	_____	following directions
_____	attendance	_____	personal hygiene/self care
_____	punctuality	_____	other _____

*Utilizing all skills with a rating of 6 or above, list opportunities within the school program that seem appropriate for the listed competencies:

_____

_____

The Solution-Focused Individual Education Plan *(continued)*

D. Academic/Developmental: (Grade or age levels alone are not sufficient)

1a. *_____ Indicate the content areas in which the student is competent and can receive instruction in the regular or remedial program without modification:

_____ all subjects _____ reading _____ math _____ social studies

_____ English _____ science _____ spelling _____ computer lit.

_____ health _____ vocational _____ fine arts _____ physical educ.

_____ other _____

1b. *Based on the identified subjects competencies, and collaboration with the assigned teacher, list the identified subject below and a brief explanation of the **effective teaching methods identified as effective with this student:

(** individual work, group work, isolation from peers = less distractibility, individual library assignments/projects, visual stimulation, seating arranged near the teacher, parent cooperation/collaboration, journal, rewards, dates, assigned to assignments, etc.)

Subject	Effective teaching methods
_____:	_____
_____:	_____
_____:	_____
_____:	_____

2. *Indicate the content areas in which the student's competency development needs assistance from a special educational program:

_____ all subjects _____ reading _____ math _____ social studies

_____ English _____ science _____ spelling _____ computer lit.

_____ health _____ vocational _____ fine arts _____ physical educ.

_____ other _____

3. *List the subject areas from #2 in which the student needs additional assistance from special education to further develop competencies leading to mastery. Also list appropriate, effective teaching methods from #1b above, which would lead to more competent performance:

Subject	Effective teaching methods
_____:	_____
_____:	_____
_____:	_____
_____:	_____

Brainstorming Toward Solutions

For School Problems

1. **Complaint:** What the student is *not* capable of doing what keeps him from succeeding in school. Example: He is not able to read past a first-grade level.

_____

_____

_____

2. **Resolution of complaint:** What the student would be doing in the near future in his classrooms so that he is more successful. (Describe what those actions would *look* like.) Example: He would be reading on grade level.

_____

_____

_____

    A. How will this resolution assist the student to function later in his life? (What will it do for him as a person, as an adult in society?) Example: He would be able to read the newspaper, follow directions, drive a car, write a check, fill out a job application.

_____

_____

_____

_____

_____

_____

_____

_____

_____

Brainstorming Toward Solutions *(continued)*

B. Besides academic success, how does this student learn? How did he learn to tie his shoes, remember when recess starts, recall small amounts of information? How does he learn best? Example: He is a visual learner. He also must repeat a task over and over to remember how to do it. He likes structure and does best with a strict routine.

_____

_____

_____

_____

_____

C. If this student is not able to perform to the preferred grade level, what are some alternatives that can help the student to accomplish the answer to B? Example: We can lower expectations of higher reading abilities and focus on lesson plans that reinforce—over and over—basic words for grades 1–4. We can visually add actions to the lesson plans so that the student associates the words with actions, since he learns best by reinforcement and visual aids.

_____

_____

_____

_____

_____

D. How can the teachers in the student's system begin to work within the student's academic deficits towards the goals described here? Example: When they give him assignments in class they should modify them to the appropriate grade level, add visual stimulation to keep his attention, make the assignments meaningful, and add additional work to push him further one time per week.

_____

_____

_____

_____

_____

Chapter Five Practice Exercise

A Different Type of Intelligence

Read the following excerpt and notice how each boy approaches the same challenging problem differently.

> Two boys are walking in a forest. They are quite different. The first boy's teachers think he is smart, his parents think he is smart, and, as a result, he thinks he is smart. He has good grades, and other good credentials that will get him far in his scholastic life. Few people consider the second boy smart. His test scores are nothing great, his grades aren't so good, and his other credentials are, in general, marginal. At best, people would call him shrewd or street-smart. As the two boys walk along in the forest, they encounter a problem—a huge, furious, hungry-looking grizzly bear, charging straight at them. The first boy, calculating that the grizzly bear will overtake them in 17.3 seconds, panics. In this state, he looks at the second boy, who is calmly taking off his hiking boots and putting on his jogging shoes.
>
> The first boy says to the second boy, "You must be crazy. There is no way we are going to outrun that grizzly bear!"
>
> The second boy replies, "That's true. But all I have to do is outrun you!"

Both boys in that story are smart, but they are smart in different ways. The first boy quickly analyzed the problem, but that was as far as his intelligence took him. The second boy spotted the problem, but he also came up with a creative and practical solution. He displayed successful intelligence. (Sternberg, 1997, pp. 40–41)

Question for discussion

How many students similar to the "second boy" are you teaching now? What will be different for you and them when you begin to notice their "successful intelligence" more often? How will it affect the way you teach and relate to them? How do you imagine that it will impact the way they view themselves as students?

*Write a note to one of your "second boys" today, describing something the student did that showed his unique intelligence. Address it to him and to his parents.

Chapter Six
Learning to Think Differently about the Student with a Diagnosis

"Nothing in life is to be feared. It is only to be understood."

—Marie Curie

Just three weeks ago she was on task, raising her hand and chattering away with the other fifth-grade students. She ran relays on Field Day just a month ago. She excelled in the fundraiser that would take her and her schoolmates to the amusement park in the spring. Her grades were all "A's" and her citizenship grade was superior. Why, then, is Lizzie suddenly not completing her work, talking back, sleepy in the morning, and fussy in the afternoon? Is she defiant? Has something happened at home? Could she be depressed?

… A month ago the senior who sits in your AP English class was writing exceptional poetry and essays. He was chosen as "Most Likely to Succeed" and he always had his girlfriend at his side in the hallways, smiling and carrying on in his typical friendly manner. For the past several weeks you have become concerned about his lack of interest in the class. He lacks motivation and seems unwilling to compromise on completing work that, if left undone, will cause his average to drop ten points. He has been absent more often than before. Has he developed "senior-itis"? Has he become too distracted with the job he has on the weekend? Is the girlfriend taking up too much of his time? Could *he* be depressed?

… The kindergartner began the school year by listening to your every suggestion and obeying your rules. She played with her classmates and was always commended for sharing. She loved to color and listen to stories. When she began to strike other children and refuse to sit still, you were astounded. You tried to calm her, but she pulled away from you and cried. Her mother talked to you in a conference and said that she had noticed her daughter being more difficult to handle at home since she and the girl's father separated a month ago. Has the child taken the divorce too personally? Is she angry? Could a young child be depressed?

Understanding the facts behind the diagnoses

Typically when a child's or adolescent's behavior changes drastically, concerned and frightened parents request the name of a professional from their family physician or school counselor who can help them understand what is causing their child to act and

149

react differently. After an assessment of symptoms and description of the various changes in behavior, a diagnosis is usually given to explain the cause or the change in behavior. Parents take the information as a resource for understanding. Often their child or adolescent is given medication as a tool to control the symptoms and hopefully regain quality in their life.

Sometimes when the child returns to school, the school counselor speaks with the parent(s) and learns about the diagnosis that has been given to the student. That's where things often stop, unfortunately. Some parents like to keep their children's problems private, which is certainly understandable. However, when teachers *are* told by

parents or the school counselor that a student in their classroom has been diagnosed by a professional, it is helpful to have some sort of knowledge of what to expect from the student as recovery happens. It is also helpful for the solution-focused teacher to have the information so that she can assist parents in identifying *exceptions* to the symptoms. Being able to point out, for example, to a parent of a depressed sixth grader that the student seemed brighter and was able to concentrate better on Thursday gives hope to the parent. The teacher can support the student better during their six-hour day together when she has some simple knowledge about the student's diagnosis, then uses a solution-focused *attitude* to assist the student in overcoming the symptoms.

Thinking about the diagnosis as just another language

Chapter Six will attempt to provide information about the various diagnoses typically given to children and adolescents. While teachers should never suggest that a child has an anger problem, eating disorder, drug or alcohol dependency, ADD (Attention Deficit Disorder) or is depressed, what a teacher *can* do is suggest to a parent that the child or adolescent seems "off track", or "not himself lately". The teacher can then suggest that the parent speak to the school counselor and receive information on where to go for additional help.

In addition, this chapter will briefly explore the various types of learning disabilities that are discussed in special education meetings or parent meetings so that teachers can understand the "language" shared by everyone involved. Keep in mind while reading this chapter that the information given is simply another way of explaining behavior and individual differences in learning. The information is important and real, yet the solution-focused teacher does not allow the descriptions to inhibit her expectations of students; she simply keeps it in mind so she can watch for exceptions to it. Since behaviors and symptoms do not occur constantly, Chapter Six will also give you guiding solution-focused ideas so that you can recognize more readily the symptom-free times. From the material on learning disabilities, teachers can gather ideas that will enhance the student's learning capacity in the regular classroom. Take the information in this chapter and use it as one tool, never forgetting that the solution-focused teacher has many tools to choose from, yet *always* chooses the tool that works.

Major Depressive Disorder—understanding the sadness

People become sad when sad things happen to them. Feeling sad is normal. Sometimes when sadness takes over a person's life after a traumatic event such as a death, job loss, divorce or illness—and is prolonged—it is referred to as depression. When children become sad because of a loss or a major change in their lives, they sometimes act out or seem hyperactive in a manner that is inappropriate to their normal behavior. When adolescents become sad over a situation, they sometimes take risks with substances, activities, and may even consider suicide as a cure. In other words, no matter what age a person is, depression affects their lives in an unkind manner, influencing them to not participate in life as they did before.

Diagnostic symptoms of major depression

The following symptoms describe some behaviors you may see in children and adolescents who are described as depressed. Five (or more) of these symptoms have been present during the same two-week period and represent a change from previous functioning; at least one of the symptoms is either (1) depressed mood or (2) loss of interest or pleasure (*Desk Reference The DSM-IV*, pp. 161-163).

- Depressed mood most of the day, nearly every day, as indicated by either subjective report (e.g., feels sad or empty) or observation made by others (e.g., appears tearful); note: Can be irritable mood in children and adolescents
- Markedly diminished interest or pleasure in all, or almost all, activities most of the day, nearly every day
- Significant weight loss or weight gain when not dieting, or decrease or increase in appetite nearly every day
- Insomnia or hypersomnia nearly every day
- Psychomotor agitation or retardation nearly every day (observable by others, not merely subjective feelings of restlessness or being slowed down)
- Fatigue or loss of energy nearly every day
- Feelings of worthlessness or excessive or inappropriate guilt nearly every day

- Diminished ability to think or concentrate, or indecisiveness, nearly every day
- Recurrent thoughts of death (not just fear of dying), recurrent suicidal ideation without a specific plan, or a suicide attempt or a specific plan for committing suicide

Suggestions for teachers

Watch for times when the student is not so depressed and note the social situation, activity, or assignment in which he or she participated slightly better. Repeat similar assignments whenever possible. It is not necessary to say anything about how much better the student looks or acts; that only draws attention to the fact that a problem exists or existed. Instead, simply compliment on the assignment and mention, "How were you able to finish that so easily? You are truly amazing!" These are the same questions that appear throughout this book. Just because depression is bothering the student does not mean that the strategy needs to differ. It will be more helpful to the student to see herself as normal than to view herself as "depressed". If you hear of a child or adolescent talking about suicide, *always take the student seriously*. Talk briefly to him or her about what you heard and ask if he or she has a plan. This is very important to adolescents, whose future scope is so short. If the student describes a plan, gently suggest that you and he go talk to a counselor then. If the student says that she has no plan but is just sick of life, suggest to the student that perhaps talking to someone would help her feel better. Let her know that you would like to mention to the school counselor that a talk sounds helpful.

Oppositional Defiant Disorder—when kids are too bold

Ask any professional who works with children or adolescents what type of diagnosis he or she would give to an acting out, talking back, disobedient, and defiant adolescent and it would be Oppositional Defiant Disorder. Yet typically, the student who exhibits these traits is not oppositional with everyone. There is usually one teacher, one coach, or a cafeteria worker who gets along with the student. The manner in which those persons interact with the student are clues to helping a student with this disorder. A person becomes defiant and oppositional when he feels powerless in his life, so when he becomes too bold people listen. Unfortunately, instead of getting the right attention he gets the wrong attention and it multiplies over time because the consequences are severe and punitive. These are often children who feel abandoned, unloved, unaccepted, and unattached to their family. They are the adolescents who are living in homes where parents don't listen and are preoccupied with their own  lives and not invested in their adolescent's. When I wrote *Parenting Toward Solutions* (1997), I interviewed fifteen adolescents and asked them what their parents did that helped them to be the happy, healthy, law-abiding citizens they were. Their answers centered around the fact that their families consistently did the following:

- always attend my sports events
- celebrate my every accomplishment
- are always "there" for me, and that, in turn, makes me there for them
- eat dinner together
- ground me if necessary, but for a short time so I can work my way back
- respect my privacy
- don't make me feel guilty like my friends' parents do
- believe in me and tell me to do what I think is right
- tell me I will be rewarded when I keep up the good work
- discipline me early and then treat me like a human being
- do what they tell me to do
- always want to know where I am

In my counseling practice, I *don't* see adolescents who come from families with these descriptions.

Diagnostic symptoms of Oppositional Defiant Disorder

The following symptoms may be seen in children or adolescents who are diagnosed as being oppositional and defiant. There is a pattern of negativistic, hostile, and defiant behavior lasting at least six months, during which four (or more) of the following are present (*Desk Reference to The DSM-IV*, p. 68).

- Often loses temper
- Often argues with adults
- Often actively defies or refuses to comply with adults' requests or rules
- Often deliberately annoys people
- Often blames others for his or her own mistakes or misbehavior
- Is often touchy or easily annoyed by others
- Is often angry and vindictive

Note: Consider a criterion met only if the behavior occurs more frequently than is typically observed in individuals of comparable age and developmental level.

Suggestions for teachers

Watch for times when the student is compliant and cooperative—even on a small scale. People are not born defiant; they develop that way when they feel powerless in their lives to get their needs met. They don't receive what the adolescents described in the earlier list, so meet their needs! We as teachers are pseudo parents. Look behind the rough exteriors of your oppositional students and see a student who has unmet needs. When you keep your stance of acceptance of even the smallest thing, the opposition will begin to melt. If you take an oppositional stance yourself, you are giving the student *more* of what he is already experiencing in other parts of his life system. I once worked with a young man who was described as being oppositional and defiant. Everyone saw only his gross behaviors, except for a nurse who said he always greeted the new patients with a warm handshake. Because of this recognition, the staff made a point to ask him to introduce others and to lead some activities. They began to notice that his oppositional behavior lessened considerably.

Attention Deficit Disorder—redirecting the energy

A wise psychiatrist once told me that a child or adolescent should never be medicated for hyperactivity; she should be medicated for an attention deficit. This diagnosis seems to be the answer given to explain why many children in elementary schools simply cannot sit still long enough to finish an assignment or read a paragraph and comprehend it. Assessing a child or adolescent for ADD should include criteria from home, outside activities, and school. If a student functions well at school and then goes home to be "hyperactive", most probably

he is not bothered by ADD. If, however, a young second grader cannot complete his work due to distractions, has a difficult time remembering what the baseball coach tells him to do, and flits from one activity at home to another, there is reason to think that ADD might be bothering him. Many children and adolescents function without medication. However, they seem to do best with very structured and patient teachers who realize the entity and cooperate with the student's need to be constantly monitored. If parents decide to give medication to their child or adolescent, watch for changes and note them so that the parents are aware of the benefits. As you compliment the student on being more successful, mention that you are glad to see such a wonderful side of him emerging or his ability to control the energy.

Diagnostic symptoms of Attention Deficit/Hyperactivity Disorder

Inattention (Attention Deficit Disorder [ADD])

Six or more of the following symptoms of inattention have persisted for at least six months to a degree that is maladaptive and inconsistent with developmental level (*Desk Reference to The DSM-IV*, pp. 63–64).

- Often fails to give close attention to details or makes careless mistakes in schoolwork, work, or other activities
- Often has difficulty sustaining attention in tasks or play activities
- Often does not seem to listen when spoken to directly
- Often does not follow through on instructions and fails to finish schoolwork, chores, or duties in the workplace (not due to oppositional behavior or failure to understand instructions)
- Often has difficulty organizing tasks and activities
- Often avoids, dislikes, or is reluctant to engage in tasks that require sustained mental effort (such as schoolwork or homework)
- Often loses things necessary for tasks or activities (e.g., toys, school assignments, pencils, books, or tools)
- Is often easily distracted by extraneous stimuli
- Is often forgetful in daily activities

Hyperactivity (Attention Deficit Hyperactivity Disorder [ADHD])

Six or more of the following symptoms of hyperactivity–impulsivity have persisted for at least six months to a degree that is maladaptive and inconsistent with developmental level (*Desk Reference to The DSM-IV*, p. 64).

- Often fidgets with hands or feet or squirms in seat
- Often leaves seat in classroom or in other situations in which remaining seated is expected
- Often runs about or climbs excessively in situations in which it is inappropriate (in adolescents or adults, may be limited to subjective feelings of restlessness)
- Often has difficulty playing or engaging in leisure activities quietly
- Is often "on the go" or often acts as if "driven by a motor"
- Often talks excessively
- Often blurts out answers before questions have been completed
- Often has difficulty awaiting turn
- Often interrupts or intrudes on others (e.g., butts into conversations or games)

Suggestions for teachers

Above all things, realize that the child or adolescent who is bothered by ADD or ADHD truly has difficulty paying attention to what you ask her to do. Notice the two different diagnoses: ADD and ADHD. Both need not be present at the same time. A third-grade girl who seems to daydream while you assign a social studies exercise needs your prompting and reminders to complete her assignment. She may sit completely still in her seat but she is in far-away-land. Believe, too, that even though she is bothered by ADD, she still may be very bright and capable. Realize that she may need to take a test in a quiet place of her choice. If she receives medication, you may see that her attention span is better and her concentration more efficient.

The first-grade boy who moves constantly as if he is "wound tightly" will need your watchful eye and structured classroom rules to help him structure and control himself—but even then, he will forget. Your understanding and patience, however, will buy you many rewards. Refer to the "energy" that bothers the hyperactive elementary child as something for him to control for five minutes. Compliment him when he is able to sit for five minutes and ask him how he was able to be bigger than the energy. Should he receive medication, you may see that he will listen to your directions longer, stay in his seat more easily, and think before he reacts.

The secondary student may feel the effects of ADD by having difficulties completing assignments quickly and neatly. Her comprehension skills may be lacking, so any help you can give by saying "Just start by reading the first two paragraphs" will guide her to focus and lessen her tendency to feel overwhelmed. Help her to look for key words as links to where she is in the passage. In math, ask her to start at the top and not worry about all of the problems. Again, patience is vital, for the adolescent will feel embarrassed at times because an assignment is hard to complete and his peers are finished before he is. Give more time on an assignment. Tell her to come in after school or at homeroom so that you can collect the assignment or assist her with any questions. She needs your direction to follow through. Give her a time and be consistent with being there and reminding her. Soon it will become a habit for her that she will appreciate. Direct, structured statements made with kindness and sincerity will earn you high points with the teen whose energy seems to make his or her life chaotic (*Desk Reference to The DSM-IV*, pp. 63–64).

Conduct Disorder and Antisocial Personality Disorder—when kids challenge society

During the past few years, children and adolescents have been killed in schools in Mississippi, Arkansas, Kentucky, Oregon, and Virginia. Questions of "why?" along with parental blame and school board discussions surrounded our grief and shock. It seemed unbelievable that a student would turn to murder to challenge his world and solve his problems. It also is important that we begin to watch for these troubled children and adolescents and not allow them to be invisible to those in their school world. We have passed the days when we can turn our heads and hope kids change. It is too late for the others but not too late for the living students in your classes.

Described here are two disorders of concern to educators. The first, Conduct Disorder, describes children primarily in prepubertal stages. The second, Antisocial Personality Disorder, describes adolescents at least eighteen years of age.

Diagnostic symptoms of Conduct Disorder

This is a repetitive and persistent pattern of behavior in which the basic rights of others or major age-appropriate societal norms or rules are violated, as manifested by the presence of three (or more) of the following criteria in the past 12 months, with at least one criterion present in the past 6 months (*Desk Reference to The DSM-IV*, pp. 66–67).

- Age at onset is prepubertal
- Often bullies, threatens, or intimidates others
- Often initiates physical fights
- Has used a weapon that can cause serious physical harm to others (e.g., bat, brick, broken bottle, knife, gun)
- Has been physically cruel to people
- Has been physically cruel to animals
- Has stolen while confronting a victim (e.g., mugging, purse snatching, extortion, armed robbery)
- Has forced someone into sexual activity
- Has deliberately engaged in fire setting with the intention of causing serious damage
- Has deliberately destroyed others' property (other than by fire setting)
- Has broken into someone else's house, building, or car
- Often lies to obtain goods or favors or to avoid obligations
- Has stolen items of nontrivial value without confronting a victim (e.g., shoplifting, but without breaking and entering; forgery)
- Often stays out at night despite parental prohibitions, beginning before age 13 years
- Has run away from home overnight at least twice while living in parental or parental-surrogate home (or once without returning for a lengthy period)
- Often truant from school, beginning before age 13 years
- The disturbance in behavior causes clinically significant impairment in social, academic, or occupational functioning

Suggestions for teachers

While some students in your classroom may exhibit some of these symptoms, hesitate to decide they are bothered by the diagnosis; instead, watch them closely and attempt to build relationships with them that are different from what they are used to. Confrontation and imposing consequences on this group rarely works well. Instead, punishment coupled with conversation, particularly the hopeful type of conversations that are solution focused, work better. I worked once with Ken, a 14-year-old male who had all of the symptoms of conduct disorder except for cruelty to animals. His parents were divorced and his mom would send him to live with his dad whenever he acted out. His life was like a pendulum, swinging from one parent to the other. When Mom brought him to counseling, she boldly said that she had had it with him and wanted a referral to send him to long-term residential treatment. I asked Mom to leave for a few minutes while I talked with her son:

LM: Mom has told me some things about you but I am interested in what you have to say.

Ken: What do you want to know, how bad I am?

LM: Is that how people see you?

Ken: Yes.

LM: What do you do that throws them off, thinking you're bad?

Ken: The stuff I do. I run away at night, steal, do drugs, sell drugs, you know, you heard all she said about me. It's true. Then my Dad. What a joke. I have to live in this barn type house in the back of his house when I'm there. Sometimes I smoke in it and that really gets him. I don't care, though. They don't care about me either.

LM: What do you wish your mom and dad would see in you?

Ken: That I'm good. (He begins to sob very hard.)

LM: OK. Tell me what the good Ken would be doing when Mom and Dad noticed.

Ken: I used to be an honor student. Now I have to go to summer school. I could pass if I wanted. I used to. I'd like to get along with my mom at her house. My brother hates me, though, and she's turned my grandparents against me, too.

Ken described to me what many adolescents want from the families and don't get, yet being inexperienced in the world without a supportive system *anywhere*, they go haywire and Conduct Disorder becomes an explanation. Talking to Ken as I did, I was able to talk to his mom and dad, and ask Ken to show them, just for a week, the "good Ken". I told him to do whatever it took to show them the difference. I asked Mom to hold on and resist her punitive strategies just for a week and watch for Ken's improvement. Mom and Ken returned the next week and Mom reported a complete turnaround for Ken. This change lasted for three months, until Ken returned to school. In Chapter Seven, I will detail what happened to Ken when he returned to school in the Fall.

More about personality disorders

Persons diagnosed with personality disorders show a consistent pattern of behaviors that deviate markedly from those other persons in the individual's culture. Their way of perceiving and interpreting themselves and others and events is *different*, resulting in behaviors that are odd and offensive to others. Their perceptions and interpretations of people and events in their lives, their emotional responsiveness to others, interpersonal relationships, and impulsivity are inflexible and pervade over many variants in their lives. Because of this pervasiveness, persons have difficulties in their social life, occupation, and personal relationships.

Diagnostic symptoms of Antisocial Personality Disorder

There is a pervasive pattern of disregard for and violation of the rights of others occurring since age 15 years, as indicated by three (or more) of the following symptoms (*Desk Reference to The DSM-IV*, pp. 279–280).

- Failure to conform to social norms with respect to lawful behaviors as indicated by repeatedly performing acts that are grounds for arrest
- Deceitfulness, as indicated by repeated lying, use of aliases, or conning others for personal profit or pleasure
- Impulsivity or failure to plan ahead
- Irritability and aggressiveness, as indicated by repeated physical fights or assaults
- Reckless disregard for safety of self or others
- Consistent irresponsibility, as indicated by repeated failure to sustain consistent work behavior or honor financial obligations
- Lack of remorse, as indicated by being indifferent or rationalizing having hurt, mistreated, or stolen from another

Suggestions for teachers

Being aware of the symptoms described is important to the safety of your students. Children and adolescents bothered by these two disorders may be in your school. If a student exhibits several of the serious symptoms, talk to your school counselor or vice principal and request that they talk to the student's parents. Don't accuse—simply explain your concern. If no one pays attention, copy this material and go back to your school administrator and document that you are concerned. Whenever you meet with your team or colleagues, mention your concerns so that you can all try strategies with these students that will help them vent in more appropriate ways. See these students as being angry at the world, not just the school. Don't become part of their anger by confronting them, threatening them, or punishing them to prove a point. They will simply not respond as other students will. Realize that symptoms of Antisocial Personality Disorder can be quite difficult to resolve. Stay cautious but calm. Watch for times when the student seems to be less challenging and note the situations in which those behaviors occur. Try to compliment and comment on the progress at that point and repeat such assignments or activities when possible. Students of this sort do well with mentors from the community or mentor teachers such as coaches who carry influence and a sense of authority in a positive manner.

Separation Anxiety and School Phobia—sometimes it's just so hard to leave

I once spoke with a young first-grade teacher about a mom who had difficulties getting her daughter to get out of the car when she dropped her off at school. The parent would always bring the daughter into the school, reluctantly. When she arrived at the classroom, the young daughter would go in, tearfully looking back. The teacher always reassured the mom that her daughter was fine after five minutes. As we talked, it occurred to me that perhaps what the daughter needed the mother to do, the mother was providing, although reluctantly. I suggested to the teacher that she call the mother and ask her to tell her daughter that she enjoyed walking her to her classroom each day and that she would do it for as long as she wanted her to. Several weeks after the mom began walking her daughter into the school building, the young girl told her mother one morning that she could walk in by herself.

Sometimes we need to cooperate with what students are needing. Clinging is an indicator of a child needing attention and to feel safe. The more we push them aside, the greater the need grows. As you read the list of symptoms of Separation Anxiety and School Phobia, notice how simple it would be to reassure a child consistently, almost too often, that her parent will be back in ___ minutes, hours, this afternoon, etc. Go to the window and point to the direction of the road on which the parent will arrive later.

For cases of school phobia, think how important it will be to notice when an adolescent does come to school and what he seems to participate in when he's there. Avoid saying "Joey, I'm so glad you chose to join us at school today." Instead, say, "Joey, I'm so glad you're here today. Let's go over some things you missed. You can complete them slowly and I'll help you." Often teens are reluctant to go to school when they are worried about their parents' problems. While you can do little to solve home problems, listen to your student if she decides to talk. Restrain from advice giving; just keep saying how incredible it is that she came to school in spite of the problems and took a break from the problems. Inquire, if possible, about what you and other teachers can do to make school a place where she wants to be more often.

Diagnostic symptoms of Separation Anxiety and School Phobia

The duration of separation anxiety is at least four weeks and the onset is before age 18. It is developmentally inappropriate and excessive anxiety concerning separation from home or from those to whom the individual is attached, as evidenced by three (or more) of the following (*Desk Reference to The DSM-IV*, pp. 75–76).

- Recurrent excessive distress when separation from home or major attachment figures occurs or is anticipated
- Persistent and excessive worry about losing, or about possible harm befalling, major attachment figures
- Persistent and excessive worry that an untoward event will lead to separation from a major attachment figure (e.g., getting lost or being kidnapped)
- Persistent reluctance or refusal to go to school or elsewhere because of fear of separation
- Persistently and excessively fearful or reluctant to be alone or without major attachment figures at home or without significant adults in other settings
- Persistent reluctance or refusal to go to sleep without being near a major attachment figure or to sleep away from home
- Repeated nightmares involving the theme of separation
- Repeated complaints of physical symptoms (such as headaches, stomachaches, nausea, or vomiting) when separation from major attachment figures occurs or is anticipated

Suggestions for teachers

Think back to a time when you missed someone. How did you compensate for their absence? Many of us reminisce, some of us look at pictures, and many of us just get sad. We miss the person and when they call us or write a letter the world seems whole again.

When children have difficulty breaking attachments to their parents, particularly in the elementary school, it is helpful to acknowledge that attachment and give them the means to feel comfortable. As the case study suggests, the parent who gives the extra time to walk up the steps to the school building, down to the classroom, and waves goodbye at the door is giving the child what she needs. On rare occasions when the student is still tearful as the parent leaves, ask the parent to leave something of his or hers for the child to keep until the child sees the parent at the end of the school day. Show the child the clock and physically show how the hands on the clock will move to the afternoon, a time when he or she will see Mom or Dad. Recognizing the child's difficulty and providing extra time with the student will gain the teacher some cooperation with the student. Telling the student "I will stay near you today until the school day is over" will give the student some support.

In addition, parents can be quite helpful when you ask them to think about other times when the child has transitioned to a new situation. Ask them to tell you what they did that seemed to soothe the child. Use those strategies in the classroom. I once worked with a young second grader who missed his father desperately when his parents divorced. His father moved several miles away and his mother took him to school each day. The mother told the teacher that the boy was quite happy at home because he could call his dad whenever he wanted and his dad was always happy to hear from him. The teacher was acutely sensitive to the situation and told the boy that at recess each morning he could call Dad at work. Dad agreed happily. The child called Dad approximately three mornings and thereafter, only occasionally. Knowing that he could call Dad was always an option and soon, the need to talk to him lessened. Look at separation difficulties not as a deficit, but as a need to feel close to someone.

Helping the abused student to gently step out of the story

When a child grows up, he looks to his family for support, love, and encouragement. Under normal functional circumstances, such a support system will produce a confident, motivated, and enthusiastic person ready to meet life's demands. What happens when these needs are not met? The child turns to outside influences in an effort to meet his needs.

Child abuse is a very serious problem. In 1985, over 19 million reports of child maltreatment of all sorts were filed in the United States (American Humane Association, as cited in U.S. Bureau of the Census, 1989). In a more recent national sample of families in the United States, almost 11% of the children had reportedly been kicked, bitten, punched, beaten up, hit with an object, or threatened with a knife or a gun by their parents in the past year (Wolfner & Gelles, 1993). Another national survey conducted in 1991 found that more than 400,000 American children a year are coerced into oral, anal, or genital intercourse (Finkelhor & Dziuba-Leatherman, 1994), usually by a father, a stepfather, an older sibling, or another male relative or family friend (Trickett & Putnam, 1993). It is not a pretty picture, is it? (Shaffer, 1996, p. 631).

Oftentimes, when parents bring their children or adolescents to talk about the trauma of abuse, they have been told that their children must retell their story to feel better. After working with sexual abuse survivors and physical abuse survivors (even verbal abuse fits here), I have learned that retelling the story often contributes to more feelings of powerlessness, blaming oneself for the abuse and resentment towards persons who did not *know* to rescue them from the abuse. Instead, it seems more important to assist the person with changing the perception of himself or herself from a victim to a survivor. I have found it helpful to children and adolescents to use exercises like the following one, which intends to help students see themselves as "escaping from the abuse", down the road towards freedom. Here are some questions that may help the student to find a new description of himself or herself and freedom from the label of "abused" (Metcalf, 1997, p. 186).

Check with your school counselor or administrator to see if you can talk with a student about this situation without calling the parents. Keep the student's name confidential unless you need to report current abuse to child protection services.

Clearing the path for freedom from "the event"

1. Mention that you are impressed that in spite of the "event", your student continued to live his or her life, participate in activities, and not allow the abuse to take him or her away from all of that. Ask:

   "How were you able to do that?"

2. Draw a line, such as the one below. Notice on one end is "birth" and the opposite end is "80 years". Place an "X" on the line approximately where the abuse occurred:

   birth _____X_____80 years

   Then say:

   "I'm going to draw a line. On one end I'm going to put your birthday. Tell me, about how long do people live in your family? (80 years, perhaps) Now, how old were you when this 'event' stopped? I'm going to put a mark at that point. What shall we call the 'event' that bothered you?"

   Suggestions: a trap, a black cloud, a jail. Place the name above the "X". From this point on, refer to that name.

   "What I want you to do for a moment is to imagine with me that in your mind, you are 'stepping out of the _____.' (name) As you do this, I want you to see that from this point on, you have (60–70) years left to never return to the _____. As a matter of fact, you have already moved this far …: (point from the day the abuse stopped to the current time, approximately).

   "As you imagine stepping out of the _____, how will this free you? What will you get to do in each day of your life that you move farther and farther away, never going backwards? What will others see you doing?"

3. Set goals with the student by asking:

   "During the next week, if I were to watch you, what would I see you doing that would tell both of us that you had stepped away from the _____ just a little bit?"

These questions assist the child or adolescent to visually emerge from the "event" and move onward toward life without so much influence from the event. After talking with your student using these questions, watch for any times when he or she "escapes" from the event and seems to be getting back into life. Consider writing a card or letter to your student, such as the one here:

Dear Susan,

As I watched you play with Stephanie yesterday, I noticed how happy you seemed. Obviously, you are much stronger than the "event" (name) ever was. It was nowhere to be found! I'm happy and very impressed with you. I look forward to your telling me how you have grown so much stronger!

From,

LM

The student who experiences the loss of a loved one

As with all of us, when students lose someone important to them through death, they go through a natural grieving process. Many times people think that *enough is enough, you must go on now*. While it makes sense to continue one's life and progress normally, it is also helpful to cooperate with the sadness that is happening and help the child or adolescent to recall what he or she loved about the person who has died. In the following questions, teachers can sit with a student and empathize through mutual discovery, the wonderful attributes of a person, and their positive influence on the student's life. Then, after conversing, the student can make a small contract with the teacher to live the afternoon or the next day as if the loved one was watching him or her go through the day slightly happier.

Regaining happiness through remembering

(Adapted from White, 1988, p. 30)

1. "I know how much you miss _____. I miss him/her too. I remember so many wonderful things about him/her. If you looked through _____'s eyes for a minute, what would you see in yourself that you could appreciate?"

2. "What do you think might happen if you began to appreciate this in yourself right now?"

3. "What do you think about or remember when you 'bring alive' the enjoyable things that _____ knew about you? What do you remember doing when he/she enjoyed watching you do those things?"

4. "What if you were to live in this 'influence' (or good memory) of _____ for a day or so and you imagined him/her enjoying watching you again … what might I see you doing?"

5. "What difference would it make when you began doing these things again?"

6. "What do you think others would see when you 'reclaimed' some of the discoveries that _____ enjoyed watching you do?"

7. "On a scale of 1–10, with 10 being 'you are feeling the happiest' and 1 being 'you feel very sad', where were you today before we talked? Where are you now?" (For a very young child, suggest that he/she hold out his/her arms fully for a 10 and close together for a 1.) "What did we talk about that seemed to help?"

After the teacher talks with the student, she can ask the student where he is on the scale. If the student falls backwards slightly, ask how he was able to move upward two days ago, for example. The teacher adds her own observations of what she saw him do when he seemed happier and—whenever you notice him participating in activities that his loved one would have appreciated—verbalize your discovery with him.

The student with a learning disability

What do all of the following persons have in common?

Thomas Edison

Leonardo da Vinci

Albert Einstein

Winston Churchill

Woodrow Wilson

Hans Christian Andersen

George Bernard Shaw

Cher

Tom Cruise

Henry Winkler

Each has had a learning disability and each has found his or her way in the world successfully by concentrating on his or her *abilities* rather than disabilities. Sounds like they were all solution focused, doesn't it?

Searching for "ability" in learning disability

In every classroom there are many children who learn differently. "A few years ago research showed the teacher–pupil relationship was the most important gauge of school success. Today, because of the decline in the amount of time parents spend with their children, it is the quantity and quality of the parent–child relationship that is most critical. ... When parents are dysfunctional or barely functionally literate themselves or are too busy or too stressed to help, the prognosis for the child's success becomes more bleak" (Harwell, 1995, p. 13).

As discussed in Chapter Five, the teacher's greatest challenge is to reach and teach all of her students so that they become competent in their subject matter. To do this to her best ability, the solution-focused teacher watches for the abilities in children and adolescents described as "learning disabled" and capitalizes upon them so that the disabilities transform into abilities. "Learning Disability (LD) has been called the 'invisible' handicap. Its victims do not look different; they have near-average, average, or above-average intelligence; and their hearing and vision are normal. Yet they have troubles the rest of us do not experience" (Harwell, 1995, p. 289). The solution-focused teacher is aware of learning disabilities, yet does not allow their existence to trap her into expecting less from her students. In fact, she expects more. She expects the student to achieve in spite of his diagnosis. "Research clearly shows that parents of most learning disabled children expect less of their children academically than do parents of nonhandicapped children" (Chapman & Boersma, 1979). The solution-focused teacher uses his time wisely by planning for the entire class and then adding additional interventions in his lesson plan to account for those who need extra assistance. The solution-focused teacher does not think of such planning as *extra work*; he thinks of it as a way to clarify his plan for everyone. By incorporating various ways of presenting a topic, he teaches for competency—and everyone benefits.

The following list is compiled from *Ready-to-Use Information and Materials for Assessing Specific Learning Disabilities* (Harwell, 1995, p. 289). The list contains the various types of learning disabilities commonly diagnosed and discussed in team and intervention meetings for students. Below each category are suggestions for the solution-focused teacher to use, developed from Ms. Harwell's suggestions. Notice how the interventions build on the exceptions and abilities rather than the deficits of the students. Create your own when you recognize the learning disabilities of your students. Share your discoveries with your team and the child's or adolescent's parents.

Characteristics of learning disabilities

Visual perceptual deficits
The child's visual acuity is normal, but the mind misinterprets what is seen. Some examples are letter reversals (b/d) or sequencing errors (was is called saw and vice versa). These children almost always have difficulty learning to read and may have trouble copying.

Visual motor deficits

The child has trouble making the muscles do what he or she wants them to do. The child may be awkward, accident prone, and have illegible handwriting.

Solution-focused strategies

As you give your students help for dealing with these visual perceptual and visual motor deficits, watch for their success and verbalize it immediately. Mention their neatness and attention to detail. Send a note home when they are successful. Call on them when you know they are informed about the subject matter so that they can share their knowledge with the class. Help them to describe what they see by asking, "What else do you see? What else?" Let them know when they are keen observers. Give them special projects that involve their looking for pictures and then describing the pictures with words.

1. Since the student's mind misinterprets, cooperate with his need to reinforce correct perceptions. Attach a visible strip to the student's desk and notebook so there is a model of symbols you are currently teaching. Help the student to look at the models often, pointing to them as you walk by his desk while instructing the other students in the class.

2. If the student has difficulty writing the model, ask her to draw it on the board about a foot high and go over it about 25 times. If she enjoys coloring, ask her to color a large letter and then color around the letter with different colors. This will help her to trace over the letter and understand the shape.

3. Encourage the student to use a bookmark during reading. Make one for yourself and discuss how helpful you find the bookmark in keeping your place. Watch for times when the student keeps the bookmark in place correctly. Ask her how she does so. Compliment her on her ability to follow along even if you are coaxing her as you read next to her. A good bookmark, according to Harwell, is about six inches long and one inch wide with a one-inch dark line in the center. The dark line is placed under the word the child is reading as he or she moves the marker left to right.

4. If a child has difficulty with vision, recommend an eye examination. Other helpful suggestions by Harwell include reproducing copies on blue, tan, or green paper. This reduces the amount of light from white paper. Using transparent, nonglare plastic in a color can also help the student to concentrate better.

5. If the student has trouble copying from the board, seat him closer to the board. Show the student how to look at a word on the board and remember 2-3 letters, such as syllables, to conserve time. Show him how to hold his place in a book with his index finger.

6. Notice whenever the student produces a neater-looking paper or project. Display it and let her know how impressed you are that she took her time. Ask her: "How were you able to go slow and do your work so carefully so that you barely erased?"

Auditory perceptual deficits

The child may have difficulty understanding what is said and may not be able to distinguish between similar sounds. Children with this problem are really going to have trouble in school since so much of what we learn depends on listening.

Solution-focused strategies

Watch for actions or words that gain the student's attention and repeat those actions often when you are ready to talk to her. Ask the student to give you a key sentence so that she knows when it is time to pay attention. For example, teach the student to listen and look at you when you say, "It's time to look at my eyes." In addition, the following interventions are helpful.

1. For a secondary student, supplying her with notes (copy yours!) is very helpful.
   It has long been said that a visual, auditory, and tactile lecture or lesson is best since it touches all types of learners. One of the students I worked with told me he always did well in classes where outlines were given out. He said it helped him to know what points were the most important ones to understand. When I do workshops, I give my participants outlines that I follow exactly and I use overheads to emphasize key points on the outlines. This technique allows me to explain the same item in several ways.

2. Speak slowly. Ask the student how slow you need to speak so that he understands better. Ask him where he thinks he should sit so he hears you better. Ask him what he thinks he could do to remember what you say. Perhaps teaming him up with a buddy or a peer who he seems to get along well with would be helpful. Give both of them tasks to do. Ask your student to give you a signal if he is off track and needs repetition.

3. Tape record your class lectures if you are a secondary teacher and ask the student to listen to the tape again in homeroom or study hall. Ask the student how she remembers items in other classes. Ask her what other teachers have done in the past to help her listen to directions and remember information.

4. This student will appreciate your use of visual aids, highlighted words and definitions, and emphasizing key words. Teach him to develop his own key words with a buddy. Perhaps the student can write down the words while the buddy says them to him. This will assist the student in hearing the word and writing it at the same time.

5. When showing a video to your class, hand out a sheet with five simple questions that will be answered as the video plays. Give ten extra points on the next test to those who complete all of the answers.

Memory deficits

The child has difficulty remembering what is seen or heard. This results in poor language development and low general information funds. Children with this problem do not learn information that is encountered incidentally. They require drill to retain facts. They also forget and lose things.

Solution-focused strategies

1. Play memory games such as "Concentration". Do the following exercise to intrigue your class into listening more often. Pick an interesting newspaper article out of the daily news. Tell your class that you are going to read a short article and to listen closely. Read the article and then ask five prepared questions. Have the students write down the answers. Make the questions easy and difficult. Award a $1 bill to the student with the most correct answers. Tell the class that from time to time you will be doing this exercise and it will always be a surprise (Scannel, p. 115).

2. Teach the secondary student to highlight, outline, and summarize information. Pair her with a peer and assign them to do the outline together.

3. Help the poor speller to remember his words by using verbal rehearsal. For example, in a word such as *satisfy*, the student's self-talk should go something like this: "I can hear the *s*, I can hear the *a*, I can hear the *t* … s-a-t spells *sat*. I see the word is. I can hear the *f*. The *y* sounds like an *i* but it's spelled with a *y*. Hmmm … satis-f-y spells *satisfy*." This activity is modeled daily with different words until students internalize it. Self talk done out loud will help them to learn and retain spelling (Harwell, p. 83).

4. For the elementary or middle school child, give the parents a list of what needs to be learned. Ask the parent to contact you during the next week with any discoveries of how the parent was able to help the child learn the material.

5. Commit to yourself and to your student. Realize that the student can learn but may require an enormous amount of resourcefulness on your part. Realize, too, that he or she may be but a few of the many students who learn more efficiently. Helping those students who have difficulties will result in a smoother running class.

Spatial deficits

The child lacks a sense of space and direction. He or she may get lost in familiar circumstances. This deficit may be reflected in the child's writing (cannot write on a line, letters collide with each other, or there is no space between words).

Solution-focused strategies

1. Watch for times when the student knows where he is and observe how he learned to identify his surroundings by asking him. For example, on the way to the bathroom, ask the student to show you how he knew where to go.

2. Put an arrow on the student's desk that points to the right. Show the student that she is to begin on the left side and proceed in the direction of the arrow.

3. When a student has difficulties writing down her words so that there are spaces in between, ask the student to tell you her sentence and then draw spaced-out lines so that each word has enough spaces for the letters (Harwell, p. 80). For example:

   The boy went for a walk.

   _ _ _   _ _ _   _ _ _ _   _ _ _   _   _ _ _ _.

4. The student can learn to be more organized if you watch how he organizes some activities. Ask him, "How did you know to get out your paper and pen for math?" Develop a calendar for the student with weekly assignments. Help the student to find the day on the calendar and, when he completes the assignment, check off the day.

Conceptual deficits
The child with this disability has trouble seeing relationships between objects and has difficulty reasoning.

Solution-focused strategies

1. When you show a video to your class, keep the volume off during the beginning and ask the class what is probably happening. After they have brainstormed the possible plot or situation, turn on the volume and see who was close to being correct.

2. Show the student two objects and ask the student to describe to you the differences in the objects. For example:

   cup/mug

   avocado/pear

   briefcase/overnight case

   picture of a cradle/crib

   fork/spoon

   As the student describes to you the difference and the similarity, ask her how she knew there were differences and similarities. Ask: "What was it that you looked for to tell you if it was similar or different?"

Student Disability/Ability Brainstorming Sheet

Name of Student _____ Class _____

My Goal for Student: _____

Type of Learning Disability Suspected _____

Student Interests at School and Outside of School _____

_____

_____

Strengths of Student _____

_____

_____

Social Situations that work for the Student _____

_____

Lessons, Activities, Situations in Which the Student Succeeds _____

_____

_____

Scale: Where student is currently regarding achieving competency in this subject:

_____

1   2   3   4   5   6   7   8   9   10

Strategies for Week of _____:

1. _____

_____

2. _____

_____

3. _____

_____

3. Have the student draw or illustrate a story for a creative writing assignment instead of writing the story. Pair the student with another student who can tell him the story while he draws it.

Brainstorming new ideas

The brainstorming sheet given here will help you to identify and then strategize ways to reach the student who needs additional help. For extra assistance, send home a copy of Parent Observation of Academic Success found in Chapter Five. This will give you more information and will let parents know of your diligence in assisting their child or adolescent at school.

Concluding comments

Eleven years ago my husband and I sat in a psychologist's office and learned of one of our children's developmental problems. We were told that he would most probably have learning disabilities. He was three years old at the time. Communicating with him was difficult and his hyperactivity was difficult to control. His future flashed before our eyes and we were told the most dire of possible outcomes. We enrolled him in the Child Study Center where he attended for two years. Over those two years the teachers worked diligently with him and taught us ways to help him with the learning problems that were frustrating to him.

After two years, I enrolled him in public school, requesting a teacher who was gentle yet structured. I shared information of his past education only to his principal, in confidence. I left no materials for anyone to view. As each year passed and he began to excel, our confidence grew. On occasion his physician would suggest dropping his medication for hyperactivity and he struggled. Eventually, at age 12 our son decided that he could handle things himself.

As I write this book he has achieved being on the honor roll many times and will take his first honors courses next fall in public high school. He will be in the varsity marching band next year. When he's pounding on his drum, my heart will be pounding, too!

Chapter Six Practice Exercise

The Wizard Is Already Here

What makes a good school? *Time* magazine (October, 1998) went looking for answers. The found one of their answers in the staff at Olson Middle School in Minneapolis, Minnesota:

> Every Friday at Olson Middle School, the adults—not the children—are in uniform. Principal Shannon Griffin, her staff and faculty all wear crimson T shirts that read OLSON MIDDLE SCHOOL—DREAM MAKERS. (*Time*, 1998, pp. 65–68)

As teachers we have the power to cultivate a dream or destroy it with our words or actions. We can believe that our students can achieve in spite of learning disabilities and—when we do—we send them and their parents the same message.

How do your colleagues send messages?

_____

_____

_____

Are they problem-focused or solution-focused?

_____

_____

_____

How does it make you feel to hear their descriptions of students?

_____

_____

_____

Learn to suggest gently to your colleagues new descriptions of a student whom you have noticed recently. Watch for the atmosphere to change, reluctantly. It is easy to see the differences, the deficits, the problems. It is difficult to look for solutions. But remember, the deficits will never tell you how to get to the Wizard. Only the exceptions will show you the way.

Be a Dream Maker this week!

Chapter Seven
Disciplining to Promote Motivation

"Life is a series of lessons that must be lived to be understood."

—Ralph Waldo Emerson

Tonya had finally done it. She had cursed too many times and had refused to do her school work for the last time. The vice principal decided that it was time for Tonya to go to an alternative campus setting. She would be there for two weeks. She would attend anger-management classes facilitated by the school district's social workers, her parents would be advised to attend parenting classes, and her teachers would be notified of her whereabouts for the next two weeks. In the problem-focused school setting, Tonya would return after two weeks to a faculty who privately dreaded her return. They would enjoy the two weeks without Tonya's confrontations and would be ready to see if she had changed when she returned. The vice principal would be watching Tonya's every move so that she could carry out the consequences, if necessary. The vice principal wanted Tonya to succeed desperately. She saw potential in the young student and was troubled by her difficult home life. Tonya's parents were divorced and her mother was a drug addict. Her brother was in prison and her father scarcely saw his daughter. The vice principal had tried to befriend Tonya but she was too rebellious and angry at life to respond. When she returned to school, everyone simply hoped that *Tonya* had changed.

The solution-focused approach to discipline

The solution-focused school reacts differently to students such as Tonya. The solution-focused school staff sees alternative school as a time for Tonya to take a break from her problems and regroup in a different atmosphere. When she returns to their campus *they* will greet her with a different attitude and ask her how they can keep her on their campus. Tonya's teachers are not interested in punishing her for her past wrongdoings. They are interested in helping her to get past her poor choices and discover better ones. They could wait for Tonya to see if she made better choices. Yet they understand that adolescents do not always learn that way, particularly when their family system is as rejecting as Tonya's. Tonya needed information to change and a sense that her system supported that change. When Tonya returns on Monday, the *staff* will begin creating such a change.

The meeting of the minds

Tonya will need an additional environment to see herself differently. She will appear before the administrator and the team of teachers for a *meeting of the minds* upon her

175

return to the regular campus. They will discuss the reports from the teachers who taught Tonya in the alternative program. Those teachers were trained to notice the student's abilities and build on them, requesting extra credit work where they saw student interests. The focus of the alternative program was to give Tonya a break and a chance to start over when she returned to her school. The staff believed that building a better relationship with Tonya as she returned would help her to control her behavior and develop better academic skills. Even though they had tried to build a relationship before, they learned that when students took breaks and experienced some success in alternative school, the experience made a difference. They knew that if she felt like her system was looking for ways to change her reputation, perhaps she would believe she deserved to have a new one.

The teachers and administrative staff had always marveled at how much better disruptive students had behaved in the in-school suspension programs and how much more they studied. They saw such exceptions as information to recognize and use. They began to capitalize on the phenomenon and let it *follow* the student when she was discharged from the program. They listened to what students said about the program and what worked for them before planning the student's reentry into the regular classroom. It was common for the teachers to hear the following statements from students like Tonya:

1. "Teachers in this classroom seem to care about me. They don't yell, they help."

2. "I like it because it's quiet in this classroom and I can concentrate better."

3. "The teachers give you lots of individual attention. When I raise my hand, they come and help me."

4. "I get all of my work done because I have to ... there are rules and then I get free time to sleep or do what I want."

5. "I feel smarter here because I am forced to do the work, I get a grade and I pass."

In addition, the teachers in the alternative program filled out the observation worksheet for Tonya when she returned to the classroom after successful completion of the program.

It's not over until it's really over

In the solution-focused school, if the student is assigned to attend an in-school suspension program for two or three days to be punished for disruptive behavior, she is afterwards assigned to assist the teacher(s) whom she had difficulty cooperating with so that the relationship changes from what it was before. Before this assignment occurs, the student meets with the team of teachers who had taught her classes. There, the teacher

Observations of Student Success

Teacher's Name: _____ Date: _____

Please complete the following questions. The questions will assist the teachers of _____ (student name) to approach him/her differently as he/she returns from your program. Be as specific as possible and include your observations of which conversations and academic strategies seemed to reach the student while he/she was attending your program.

1. List the strategies that were successful in teaching this student. How did he/she learn best?

_____

_____

_____

2. What methods seemed to motivate the student to finish his/her work?

_____

_____

_____

3. What successful interventions did you use to control/contain the student's behavior?

_____

_____

_____

4. What conversational strategies did you use that seemed to "connect" with the student and lesson resistance?

_____

_____

_____

5. List any additional information that will help this student's teachers be more successful with him/her in the classroom. Use the back of this sheet for your comments.

_____

_____

_____

from the alternative program meets with everyone to share the information on the Observations of Student Success worksheet. The student's parents are invited to attend the meeting, although if they do not attend, the meeting occurs anyway with the student, and the parents are mailed the Observations of Student Success worksheet. The student is then offered a mentorship with a certain teacher who volunteers to spend personal time with the student on either a daily or weekly basis as determined by the team. The student has an intense relationship with the mentor until the team and the student determine that she is back on track with school. Instead of being isolated from her class for one to two weeks, she is placed back into the classroom sooner, hopefully with a new relationship between herself and her teachers and someone to support her daily.

If the student has prior personality conflicts with a teacher(s), her mentor teacher encourages her to sit privately with them and mutually develop a strategy that would work better for everyone in the classroom. The administrator does not participate in this portion of the program so that the teacher and student become the experts on reconciliation. Each teacher is given training on how to do this and can be accompanied by the school counselor in the meeting upon request during the first few months of the school year. The school counselor coaxes the teacher but does not give advice or suggest ideas.

The re-entry without reconciliation rarely works!

Remember Ken from Chapter Six? Remember how his behavior improved when his relationship with Mom changed? Ken had made a point to show the "good" side of him and his efforts resulted in a summer free of conflict and full of emotional well being. He changed friends, became close to his mom, visited his dad instead of staying with him, and finished summer school. He seemed to be in good spirits when his mom dropped him off at school the first day of school. He went to his first period—and then on the way to second period, he ran into the vice principal who had expelled him the previous spring. The vice principal said: "Why did you even bother to come back here? Couldn't you get a hint?" Ken left school and skipped the rest of the day. His mom called me frantically when the vice principal called her to tell her that Ken was up to his old tricks. She and I met with the principal and vice principal the next day. The principal personally went to Ken's home to apologize and talk to Ken. It was too late. Ken began to stay home and did not want to go to school even when his mom offered to transfer him. She eventually placed him in a residential treatment center for a year to help him get back on track both with school and emotionally.

Don't let this story happen at your school!

Relationship-building questions for teachers

The Rebuilding Student Success worksheet was a part of the training and reconciliation process that Tonya's teachers were given to use. The questions given here are appropriate for secondary students and may be modified for elementary students.

Suspending suspension!

Tonya's school district found that the reoccurrence of suspensions diminished rapidly, because the teachers, trained in solution-focused teaching, approached the students differently. They put aside their beliefs of students' bad qualities and searched for good qualities. The students soon became less resistant to the teachers and more cooperative. The district had less complaints by parents for their new project, for the parents saw the efforts as a means to work with their child, not simply punish them over and over (which obviously did not work). In simple terms, students were *taught* how to behave appropriately in school through modeling, new communication, and strategies. Their grades improved because school began to mean something more than simply doing assignments. Students felt important. Resistance and defiance weren't occurring so often any more. They were not useful or necessary to the student.

Is this for real?

Could these ideas compose the school district of the future? Yes. Is it really possible that an entire school could adopt such a novel approach and suspend its beliefs that punishment was the only road to helping students to be competent? Yes. (See Chapter Nine for Program Implementation.) These ideas could develop without huge additional costs, minimal structural changes, and teacher study of this manual. Entirely designed and implemented by individual schools or school districts, the idea of creating an environment focusing on exceptional teaching enlists *everyone's* input and competency. The idea of faculty members disciplining and reauthoring the lives of students like Tonya—

Rebuilding Student Success

Context: Place yourself in the role of assisting the student in the transition from the alternative program to the regular classroom. Talk to your student one-on-one before his or her entrance back into your class and keep the conversation future focused without references to past behaviors that placed the student in the alternative program. See the student in need of a new context to begin new behaviors. See yourself as an instigator of such new behaviors by doing something different upon the student's return to your class. Review your part in the "problem" and determine how to offer a new role to your student, seeing that your behavior will relay to the student his or her worth to you in the classroom. Maintain your professional stance, be consistent, friendly, kind, understanding, and structured. See your student as "stuck" in an old story and be determined to help the student to write a new story so that he or she feels more successful. This strategy will help you to lessen resistance between your student and yourself and allow you both to talk calmly and collaboratively.

1. *What was helpful to you while you were in the "program"?*

   _____

   _____

   _____

   _____

   _____

   _____

   _____

2. *As you come back into my classroom, I want you to know that I am not going to talk about what caused you to leave. Instead, I am interested in helping you to stay. Let's talk about what you think you could do to stay in my classroom. You are an important student in my classroom.*

   _____

   _____

   _____

   _____

   _____

   _____

   _____

Rebuilding Student Success *(continued)*

3. *What is it that I could do to help you stay in my classroom just for the next week?*

_____

_____

_____

_____

_____

_____

(Many students will not know how to answer this question because they have not been given the chance to tell their teachers what they need from them, so be patient. Continue asking. This question may be embarrassing for the student. Help the student by suggesting what the "program" teacher mentioned.)

4. *Imagine one day very soon when things are better for you in my class. We will still have assignments and work to do, but things will seem better for you. Who do you think will begin to notice how much better things are for you?*

_____

_____

_____

_____

_____

_____

5. *What do you see yourself doing that will help you to stay in my class for the next two weeks? What else? What else? What else?*

_____

_____

_____

_____

_____

_____

instead of administrative interventions—placed her systemically in the middle of the teachers she offended so that she could be seen differently by everyone, including herself. This *school district of the future* is a combination of programs that are slowly developing in today's schools. They make sense because they provide structure, limits, and listen to student needs. They capitalize on doing things that work and eliminating those that do not. The teachers and staff believe that the student needs a different context when he exits from the program in order to react differently. They are not interested in controlling the student. They are interested, however, in his controlling him- self and they believe it can be done when the environment says "you can". By presenting such a program, they increase the student's chances of success and lessen their stress.

The problem-focused school in comparison

Notice the difference in the program just described and a problem-focused school. Usually when a student returns from a punitive environment and transitions into a problem-focused school environment, he or she is told by administrators and teachers:

"Now it is up to you to stay out of this suspension program. The next time your behavior is disruptive, you will be expelled. It will happen and that's a promise!"

Notice the difference when the solution-focused school approaches the same discharge differently:

"Since you have completed the program, you now have a chance to experience something differ-ent. We are going to work with you differently as you come back into our school. We have learned the following from your teachers during your alternative experience and we are going to put those same factors to work in the classroom so you can be successful here."

Discoveries made by alternative school teachers are described and their applications in the classroom are discussed.

"We want you to know that we will not give up on you. We are too impressed with your success in the ISS program."

Imagine being that student for a moment. Which statement would inspire you to perform and behave better?

The Solution-Focused Discipline Guide Sheet

Granted, there will always be students who show behaviors that are dangerous to others. Those students fare best away from other students. The plan described earlier is a preventive program that changes the context for students who "get off track" or break too many rules. The plan places responsibility on everyone in the student's system, increasing the odds that the student will change behaviors. (See the Solution-Focused Discipline Guide Sheet on page 184.) The importance of the interventions is that the student does not have to pay over and over for what he or she did before. The student is seen as someone who got off track and is now on track again. The teachers' change of perception is contagious. Students are surprised when they are greeted by well-wishing teachers who desire for the student to learn from his or her experience *differently*. There is a nice sort of pressure to succeed when everyone seems to believe that you can.

Note: Students do not often think that teachers will change to accommodate them, particularly when it is the student who has made the infraction. (Change their minds!) Schools typically look down upon students for their misbehaviors and brand them as troublemakers, lazy, or always in trouble. By suggesting to a student that his teachers will be changing causes the student to watch more closely for such changes; thereby, the student will react differently as well. New reactions from the student will send a message to the teachers that their efforts are working. Therefore, truly impress upon the student to watch closely *and* to give the teachers a chance to see him or her like never before.

Teaming up to change the system and a student's reputation

I once had the opportunity to talk with a junior high girl, Karen, whose grades had dropped dramatically. Her parents told me that she had begun hanging out with the wrong type of crowd and had let her school work go unfinished. They had tried talking, grounding, and yelling to no avail. When I spoke with Karen she was quite sure that the

Solution-Focused Discipline Guide Sheet

Name of Student _____ Date _____

Infraction _____

_____

1. Goal of Administrator/Teacher for Student:

    _____

    _____

    _____

2. How often has this infraction occurred?

    _____

3. Look back to a time when the infractions did not occur. What was happening then? (Interview the student about his or her academic and family life.)

    _____

    _____

4. What disciplinary actions have been taken in the past?

    _____

    _____

5. Which disciplinary action changed the behavior? (Repeat those that worked. Disregard those that did not work.)

    _____

    _____

6a. Which teachers on the student's team (or other faculty member) seems to have a positive relationship with the student?

    _____

b. What does that faculty member do that seems to reach the student? (Interview the faculty member.)

    _____

    _____

Solution-Focused Discipline Guide Sheet *(continued)*

7. Student's method of staying out of trouble *sometimes*. Student's explanation of non-referrals from certain teachers. What do those teachers do that helps? (Interview the student.)

_____

_____

_____

8. Nonreferring teacher's strategy that helps the student to stay out of trouble:

_____

_____

_____

9. **New Disciplinary Strategies:** From the answers to #5–8, write the strategies that have worked with the student to change behavior. Remember to only write down those strategies that have worked, disregarding those that were not successful. Write which faculty member can help to carry out the tasks.

_____

_____

_____

_____

10. **Scale:** On a scale of 1–10, where is the student in reconciling the infraction? Show this scale to the student and ask him/her where he/she sees the progress.

no change   successful

        1   2   3   4   5   6   7   8   9   10

Ask: "What can you begin to do for this week only (secondary) or just for today (elementary) that will push you up on this scale just one step?"

Say: "While you are working on changing your behavior, your teachers are going to be watching for your changes and doing some changing themselves. I want you to watch for the changes very closely."

185

reason for her failure was that the work was just too hard. She said she couldn't keep up with the teachers and when she got behind, she could never catch up. When that happened, instead of asking for help, she began talking to her friends and misbehavior followed.

Talking with Karen, I agreed with her that a social life was indeed important. She replied that her teachers saw her as too social, since they had begun sending home notes to her mother regarding her talking back in class. Again, I mentioned that it was important to have friends, yet what really worried me was that she was giving her teachers the wrong impression of her. After all, I found her personable and kind while talking to her. I then asked her teachers to speak with Karen jointly in a team meeting and describe to her what they liked about her. While I was not present for the meeting, the teachers later told me what they said to her:

"We have always seen you as a sort of leader in our classes. We looked at your records from last year and the scores were just what we expected to see ... you have such talent and abilities. We all enjoy having you in our classrooms. Sometimes you forget to pay attention but we realize that friends are very important to you. We were wondering if you would watch for times during the next week when it was okay to talk and then when class work needed to be done. We will all be watching your leadership again. The other students certainly watch what you do. We will appreciate your help. We intend to change our ideas about you, so watch what we do that you think is different. We would like you to come back to our meeting next Friday so we can all talk about what happens next week."

Karen made a complete turnaround in a week. When she returned to the team meeting a week later, the teachers presented her homework grades to each other and were able to share their observations of how she helped their classes to stay on track. Thereafter, the team requested that Karen visit with them every other week and then eventually they ceased meeting with her when her academic scores became stable. Karen herself told me later:

"I had no choice but to change. They were all so nice. I wasn't used to teachers being so nice and asking me what they could do for me. I just always thought that they were too mad at me for what I did to care."

The team leader called Karen's parents who were delighted with the changes they had begun to see in their daughter at home. While she still did things with her new friends, she seemed to be more interested in completing her school work. The team had assisted the student in developing a new perception of her academic abilities by observing her in a different manner. Instead of observing what she was not doing, they watched for how she perceived herself and her school life. Then they went about to change her perception.

Change the student by changing the system!

The following ideas were used by Karen's teachers:

1. From listening to the student's language and observing her academic behavior in my classroom, how does she probably perceive herself?

    Example: This student seems despondent. She may think that school is meaningless for her since she rarely seems to work on any assignment. Perhaps she needs to help me at my desk today so I can compliment her on her productivity. I wonder what she would enjoy doing for me?

2. What can I say or do that might alter her perception of herself just slightly, for today?

    Example: I can compliment her on her dress, his shirt, or anything small that I notice during class. I can call on the student and ask a question about something I know he is interested in. For example, Todd has on a Boston Red Sox shirt today. I wonder if he would be interested in going to the library and looking up the history of Fenway Stadium for our history chapter on American heroes?

3. How can I step into her world view and help her to feel accepted in a small way so that I gain her respect and attention and dissolve any resistance or tendency to not perform?

    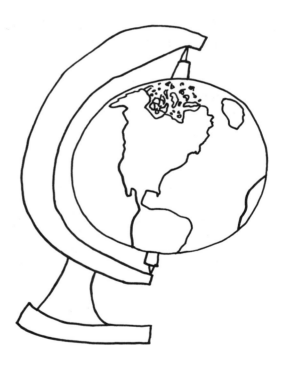

    Example: When I feel resistance from Renae, I will agree that the assignment is long and hard and suggest that she just try doing two problems within the next ten minutes. I might ask her to work with Ann who seems to be a popular classmate and see if Renae is motivated by being with someone slightly more visible. I might ask both of them to sit in the hallway or in the library so that Renae is not embarrassed in any way. I can phrase my idea as "Renae, I've been wanting to see how students work together. Would you and Ann help me with an experiment today?"

4. Who else in this student's system can use the strategy I am using with this student so that she feels different about herself?

    Example: I will ask Jimvik's vice principal to take two minutes out of his busy schedule today and come by my classroom during a time when the class is informal. I will then ask him to call Jimvik out in the hall where I can compliment Jimvik in front of the vice principal.

Concluding comments

In an article entitled "Playing by the Rules", David Ruenzel writes of a coach who turned a tough, drug-abusing high school football team into a respectful group of adolescent boys who had high standards. How did he do it?

> There has to be something about the relationship between coaches and players that motivates. But what is it exactly? And is it something classroom teachers could develop with their students? Under what conditions would student–athletes work as hard for their teachers as they do for their coaches? (Ruenzel, 1994, p. 34).

The coach, Dale Patton, grew up in a family of school teachers and taught for five years in a program for potential dropouts. He did whatever it took to motivate the students—laughed with them, talked with them, relaxed with them, and showed them movies. He stepped into their world with both feet. He came to believe in a very simple philosophy that sounds too simple: " ... that you can accomplish almost anything with students if you set high standards for behavior and performance by which you yourself abided ... Patton will not curse, grab face masks, throw clipboards or yell at officials. (Ruenzel, 1994, p. 34).

There are many coaches whose tactics for winning their team's support and loyalty can teach us about curtailing behaviors in the classrooms. Perhaps it's time to be coaches ... cheerleaders ... in the classroom!

Chapter Seven Practice Exercise

Coaching Toward Solutions

Below are two notes to fill out and give to a challenging student in your classroom and the student's parent(s). Compliment the student. Your purpose is to change the student's and parents' thinking about the student and his or her time at school. The student may be a trouble student, a student with learning differences, or a student with behavioral problems. Include any *exceptions* that you noticed during the week. Give the first note to the student and the second note to the parent(s). If the student has other teachers at school, make copies of the notes so that they may use them, too. Ask your colleagues to give out the notes to the student and parent sometime during the same week you do. Discuss the noticeable changes with your colleagues after this task is completed. If it makes a difference, continue giving the notes intermittently.

To: _____

From: _____

I am amazed at you!

_____

_____

_____

_____

_____

_____

_____

_____

_____

Teacher Signature

To: _____

From: _____

Something Amazing Has Happened at School!

_____

_____

_____

_____

_____

_____

_____

_____

_____

Teacher Signature

Chapter Eight
Teaching Social Competence in the Classroom

"Occasionally in life there are moments of unutterable fulfillment which cannot be completely explained by those symbols called words. Their meanings can only be articulated by the inaudible language of the heart."

—Martin Luther King, Jr.

Doug Cook, PhD knows personally what Dr. King meant in this quote. Last spring, as part of his doctorate research, Dr. Cook interviewed a second-grade class using solution-focused ideas and observed a small hand waving with excitement. The second grader held up his recognition sheet (a sample is included in this chapter) and said, "Dr. Cook, this is what makes me feel like a '10'!"

It was a joy to meet Dr. Cook and his staff several years ago. While visiting his school, I noticed how he acknowledged every child as he walked down the hallways. There was something magical happening at his school … and it could be summed up in the way that each teacher and staff member respected every student. The faculty persevered to seek solutions, not problems. They worked as a team to help each other when someone had difficulties understanding and coping with the needs of a student. Dr. Cook had spent many hours teaching his teachers new ways of relating and working with their students. He was so intrigued by the helpfulness of solution-focused work that he studied the effects of solution-focused exercises on the self concept of elementary students. His research concluded that there were positive gains for students when they were taught to focus on solutions, not problems. The following are two parts of his program at Riverside Elementary School in Dublin, Ohio.

Recognizing social competency in the elementary school

As part of his solution-focused program, Dr. Cook meets with classes and talks to them about various topics of social competence. The following are some ideas for teachers who desire to *teach* social competence in their classrooms, yet stay solution focused so that the students discover what works for them socially. The topics can be initiated every other week so that the students can work on goals and watch their individual progress.

- How good do I feel about myself? When are the times that I feel good about myself?

- How good am I at expressing my feelings? When did I do it last?

- How cooperative am I in groups? When was the last time I was very cooperative?

- How well do I respect other students' property? How do I do this?

- How well do I *not* fight or say something unkind when someone is not nice to me? How do I do that?

- How good am I at being a friend? What do my friends say I do that works?

- How well do I keep control of my behavior? How do I control it?

- How well do I respect what someone says even if I disagree? How do I do that?

- How good are my manners? What do I do that shows that I have manners?

- How polite am I to other people? When did I do that last?

- How well do I control saying unkind words? How do I do that?

- How well do I listen to my teacher and my friends? When did I do that last?

- How well do I refuse doing something that I know is wrong? How do I refuse?

Notice how each social competency assumes that the student *has* been slightly competent in the social skill. This is referred to as presuppositional language, a solution-focused term that simply implies that change or behaviors have happened before and  therefore will happen again. The reproducible student exercise on self concept, complete with a scale of 1–10, can be a weekly guide for students' brainstorming and identification of social skills. Elementary teachers may enlarge the worksheet as an overhead and talk about the topics together with the students, offering examples or asking the students for examples. As the teacher shows the overhead and the students fill out their individual worksheets, the teacher should complete the sentences for the student by inserting the weekly topic. For example, "Today I am at a _____ because I have done the following to *feel good about myself.*"

Each week before beginning a new topic, the teacher can pass out the previous sheets and have the students talk about their success. They can then rate themselves again to see their progress. It is also fun for the students to nominate several classmates as "10's" for the week. They must, however, explain what the students did to receive such a vote. The papers can be sent home signed by the teacher. A reproducible letter explaining the program is provided for teachers to copy and send home. Including parents in the process keeps them informed and supportive of the project.

How High Is My Self-Concept Today?

Name _____ Date _____

low									high
1	*2*	*3*	*4*	*5*	*6*	*7*	*8*	*9*	*10*

Personal Goals

1. Today, I am at a _____ because I have done the following:

_____

_____

_____

2. By the next lesson, I want to be at a _____. I will get there by doing the following:

_____

_____

_____

Class Goals

3. As a class, we are at a _____. I can help us get to a higher step by doing the following next week:

_____

_____

What are my changes from last week?

_____

_____

_____   _____

Teacher Signature   Student Signature

(Adapted from Doug Cook, PhD, Dublin, Ohio.)

School Logo Here

Date: _____

Dear Parents,

As a vital part of your child's academic and social life, the teachers in your child's school believe that being socially competent is important to learning how to be a kind, caring, and well-rounded individual. Students who feel good about themselves and others seem to cooperate well and learn better. Every two weeks during this school year, our teachers will talk about a new topic with the students, with the hope of helping them to learn proper ways of being socially competent. The following areas will be discussed:

- How do I feel about myself?
- How good am I at expressing my feelings?
- How cooperative am I in groups?
- How well do I respect other students' property?
- How well do I *not* fight or say something unkind when someone is not nice to me?
- How good am I at being a friend?
- How well do I keep control of my behavior?
- How well do I respect what someone says even if I disagree?
- How good are my manners?
- How polite am I to other people?
- How well do I control saying unkind words?
- How well do I listen to my teacher and my friends?
- How well do I refuse doing something that I know is wrong?

Your child will be asked these questions and will be encouraged to answer how he/she *already achieves* some of the competency by rating himself/herself on a scale of 1–10, with "1" meaning *low* and "10" meaning *high*. Every other week your child will bring home his/her worksheet so that you can talk to your child about the successes. We believe that all children are at least slightly successful in their social skills. Our job is to help them discover their abilities and help them to expand them.

Thank you for your support.

The Teaching Staff of _____

In addition to this effective program, it may be helpful and exciting for the principal to take part in the weekly projects by identifying once per week the class with the highest rating. Elementary students enjoy short-term goals and rewards. Perhaps the class with the highest rating could go to lunch first, go to recess first, have 30 extra minutes to play outside, or view a special video on Friday. These rewards are free, yet relay a special message of the importance of being socially competent.

Who's the most responsible of them all?

Another part of Dr. Cook's outstanding counseling program—designed to keep elementary school children on track socially—is to recognize the students when they are *caught* doing something socially competent. The following exercise is easily adapted for the elementary school and involves the entire teaching staff and administrative staff. It simply requires noticing when students are being socially competent.

How the program works

Each month a different "character-building" word is selected and announced by the principal. Students are encouraged to practice behaviors that will exemplify that word after being given examples. Teachers are then encouraged to watch students making choices in that area. Copies of the nomination form (in triplicate) are hung on every teacher's door and in various places throughout the school building. When a student is "caught" doing the character-building word, the form is filled out. One copy, a white master, is given to the child to take home; another copy, a pink one, is put in the teacher's box to be displayed in the classroom; and a third copy, a yellow one, is placed by the student in a grade-level "nomination" box that is kept in the office. Every Friday afternoon, one boy's and one girl's nomination are selected from *each* grade-level box. All of the names are then read by the principal the following Monday morning. Those students are then permitted to lead the class to lunch and recess for a time determined by the teacher. Dr. Cook then places the name of each Recognized Riversider on a wall in the lunch room, for everyone to see under a sign with the "word of the month" on it.

By the end of the year, the wall is full of names of students from kindergarten to fifth grade who have demonstrated behaviors, attitudes, etc., that are responsible for controlling and exhibiting their character in a positive manner. The program takes management, but the results are worth it. The idea of catching children performing solutions and exceptions, and becoming responsible for their own behaviors, keeps the program solution-focused and lessens punishments.

RESPONSIBLE RIVERSIDER NOMINATION

STUDENT _____

CLASSROOM TEACHER _____ DATE _____

THIS STUDENT PRACTICED _____

By _____

_____

NOMINATED BY: _____

GREAT BEHAVIOR NOMINATION

STUDENT _____

CLASSROOM TEACHER _____ DATE _____

THIS STUDENT PRACTICED _____

By _____

_____

NOMINATED BY: _____

You can reach Doug Cook, PhD, by writing to him at Scioto Ridge Elementary School, 8715 Big Bear Avenue, Powell, Ohio 43065.

Making mentoring moments happen in middle school

What do you do when you have 1,200 intermediate students (grades 5-6) from a wide range of socio-economic backgrounds who do not have enough healthy adult models to influence them in their lives? You turn to the healthy faculty members in your school and you help them make deals with each other's troubling students:

"I'll take Travis, who gives you a hard time in math, and you can take Shari, who gives me a hard time in Social Studies. You can help her to feel supported, teach her some social skills—and I'll do the same for Travis."

Judy Martin, MEd, sat back and watched her program grow from 13 mentors to over 52 mentors in three years and she's still smiling at the excitement. When a teacher coined the acronym "C.H.U.M.S" (Children Hooked Up with Mentors), Ms. Martin of Bear Creek Intermediate School in Keller, Texas knew she had an idea that would serve everyone.

The C.H.U.M.S are all here

Ms. Martin began the program by identifying children who were giving their teachers difficulties. She asked teachers from different teams to "adopt" the student and to become their mentor. To recruit the teachers, she held an informal meeting with desserts and talked briefly about what her dream was for the students she saw at risk. The mentors were asked to simply spend time with their adopted student and become a sort of pseudo parent to them. These students, she said, needed an ally on whom to depend. The students whom Ms. Martin saw benefiting the most were children with single parents, low socioeconomic backgrounds, poor social skills, and deficits in learning and hearing.

The program has grown to include activities, beginning each fall with a "Pumpkin Carving Party". The mentors record their moments in a scrapbook and enjoy treats from local merchants such as pizza, sub sandwiches, and cakes. Ms. Martin broadens the scope and fun of the project by declaring certain days "Steal Your Chum for Lunch" during which the mentor and student eat a special lunch together. Recently Ms. Martin borrowed some local high school students and taught them to be C.H.U.M.S, increasing the number of students touched by the program.

Programs such as these focus on what works for those students whose needs are not being met. As this book has promoted in other chapters, when a student's perception of himself changes, so does his behavior. Many of us behave in contexts where we feel important and valued. The C.H.U.M.S program does for students at risk what is done for many students not at risk … it gives them an adult to look up to and, in return, they are respected themselves.

You can reach Judy Martin, MEd, by writing to her at Bear Creek Intermediate School, 801 Bear Creek Parkway, Keller, Texas 76248.

Influencing the high school student

When students reach high school, it is quite difficult to *teach* social competence, although it certainly seems to be the time in their lives when their *incompetence* seems to show the most and keep their teachers from noticing their goodness!

Ms. Toy Angell encountered such a student named Angela, a tenth-grade student who disliked her teacher from the second she met her and did whatever she could to show her disillusionment. She would yank papers from her hand and roll her eyes when she would talk. Ms. Angell made a conscious effort to compliment Angela in spite of her antics. She *always* said "hello" to Angela and asked her how she was. Typically Angela did not respond at all. Gradually, Angela began to be less rude and more tolerant. Ms. Angell began teaching a lesson on Romeo and Juliet after Spring Break, six weeks after the semester had begun. Angela moved to the front row from where she had been sitting and began listening to every word Ms. Angell said.

One day, after a few days into the unit, after writing lab, Ms. Angell had fifteen minutes to get everyone to work before class was over. Angela took Ms. Angell's seat behind the podium. Ms. Angell asked Angella to tell the class about Romeo's family. She said "What?" Ms. Angell whispered to her what the answer was and she taught the class for a few minutes. The class listened and she took her seat when she was finished. Ms. Angell thanked her for helping her. A friendship blossomed. Angela went on that semester to present her folder, was awarded the best grade of the class, and did a wonderful presentation. She followed the class readings along and helped Ms. Angell when she would lose her place while lecturing.

When the semester was finished, and the students prepared to leave for summer vacation, Angela stood up one day and said:

"I want to make this announcement on behalf of Ms. Angell's seventh period class. (Turning to Ms. Angell) I didn't like you at first but now I like you and we think you are the greatest teacher and we don't want you to leave our school, ever. We combined our money and got you this napkin."

Ms. Angell
We love you
Your Seventh
Period Class

Ms. Angell had the attributes of patience, sincerity, and perseverance that accomplished something with a resistant student that most of us only dream of. How did she do it? She told me she put aside her perceptions and looked past the negative behaviors, believing that the best intervention for teachers is communication with a smile. "Everyone wants to believe that they are likable." While many secondary students can challenge that assumption, in my experience as a family therapist and teacher, it seems to be true.

Helping the high school student to be socially competent

Obviously, our modeling of appropriate behaviors and language towards students is number one in conveying the message of what is acceptable and what is not. In her book *Dangerous Minds* (St. Martin's Press, 1992), Lou Ann Johnson recognized why her troubled, defiant alternative class was so rude to her after a colleague pointed out what she had *not* been doing according to her students:

> You don't like us, Miss Johnson. You're very clever and witty and educated and you can verbally demolish us whenever you want to because you're older than we are and you know a lot more, but that isn't fair. It isn't very nice. And it isn't teaching. (Johnson, p. 40)

Ms. Johnson felt weak and realized that the student was correct. She had to put aside her educational theories and look at her audience, seeking out how to reach them in their own language. She had friends and colleagues who liked her. How could she be herself in a classroom of adolescents? The next day she addressed her class:

> I have a confession to make … I haven't been very nice to you. I'm sorry. But you haven't been very nice to me either. You put me on the defensive the very first day and I never got over it. Well, I'm over it now. The reason I made a seating chart was not to punish you or make you miserable. I made it because I want to help you be the most effective students you can be, so you can learn. Because I like you. If I didn't like you, I would let you sit in the back of the room and play cards instead of reading Shakespeare. See this little note? [It was a yellow sticky note with BE NICE written on it.] This is my reminder to be nice to you. And I'd appreciate it if you would do the same. What do you think? (Johnson, pp. 43–44)

For a few seconds, Ms. Johnson was afraid that her new approach would be as effective as the old one. Then students began answering questions and Ms. Johnson pointed out to them if they were nice or not nice:

> We ended up reading the entire second act over again, this time with more enthusiasm. … After the final bell, I sat at my desk, enjoying the sweet sound of students discussing the play. As they collected their books, they actually argued with each other about which of Shakespeare's characters was more believable. For an hour, I had been a teacher. And it was good. (Johnson, p. 44)

A Brainstorming Exercise for Secondary Teachers

According to the American School Counselor Association, the following are some of the social competencies that are essential to illustrate/teach in America's classrooms. Below, as a team or group of colleagues, read the left column describing the competencies. In the middle, write a brief description of what the students would be doing when they had that competency. On the right, write down what teachers could do to begin to encourage the actions in the middle column.

Example:

| has a positive attitude about self | Students would be motivated to learn and would exhibit such motivation by being interested in a subject. | Assess lesson plans and their usefulness in helping students to feel competent. Choose lesson plans that result in student interest. Ask students what types of lessons work. |

Competencies	**Solution Description**	**Our Task**
has a positive attitude about self	_____ _____	_____ _____
values life and other people	_____ _____	_____ _____
understands goal setting	_____ _____	_____ _____
identifies and expresses feelings	_____ _____	_____ _____
understands appropriate and inappropriate behaviors	_____ _____	_____ _____
recognizes personal boundaries of others	_____ _____	_____ _____

A Brainstorming Exercise for
Secondary Teachers *(continued)*

Competencies	Solution Description	Our Task
identifies personal strengths and assets		
cooperates well in a group communicates effectively without harsh language		
can make decisions		
can resolve conflict without fighting		
perseveres to learn		

(Adapted from *The National Standards for School Counseling Programs*, The American School Counselor Association, 1997.)

Creating the socially competent classroom

See the worksheet entitled "A Brainstorming Exercise for Secondary Teachers".

Conflict resolution, solution-focused style

 Solution-focused schools work because the focus is on exceptions, not problems. The next time a student seems distraught and hopeless, pull out the following steps for conflict resolution—solution-focused style—and watch what happens. You may see a happier student who has learned a nice way of dealing with life's troubles.

1. "This sounds really awful. How have you managed to keep things together so far?"

2. "How would you like for things to be?" Or, for dealing with more than one student: "How would you both like things to be?"

3. "Think back to a time when things were better for you" (and school worked, home was better, friends were nicer, life was better, people weren't angry) "Tell me about those times. What was different then? What did you do that was different then?"

4. "What would you suggest doing today that worked before for you? What else? What else?"

5. "How could you think about this situation differently today so that doing something different was easier?"

Notice the goal setting, exception gathering, and task development? The teacher does little but direct the resolution process. Teachers can use this approach with their class if the class is upset about an event or situation at school, or with individual students who feel comfortable confiding in them. In addition, it is a quick way for teachers themselves to get back on track when the day has been too stressful for words.

Concluding comments

The following excerpt is very important for teachers whose passion for teaching and desire to assist their students to be socially competent fills their days with perseverance:

> How do you get diverse people to move in the same direction? By creating a culture of respect.

The word "respect" is derived from the Latin "respicere", which means "to see", and creating a culture of respect starts with a special kind of vision from within the leader. He begins by looking at his own passions and self-esteem, in order to discover what makes him feel inspired and respected. When the leader feels good about himself, he becomes a more fulfilled person ... Leaders who act this way understand that we are all created equal, and that people who feel equal, and respected, are likely to perform to the best of their ability. (Rosen, p. 236)

Chapter Eight Practice Exercise

A Time to Self Focus

What are the strengths you bring to your classroom that your students want to emulate?

_____

_____

_____

_____

If you asked your students, what would they say you do that helps them to feel good about themselves?

_____

_____

_____

_____

What are your secrets to teaching conflict resolution *in the classroom* so that your students learn from your example? How effective are you at this, on a scale of 1–10?

_____

_____

_____

_____

If you could choose one student per day to make a difference with so that he/she feels differently about himself/herself, what could you think about or believe about yourself so that you would follow through?

_____

_____

_____

_____

Chapter Nine
Creating the Solution-Focused School
Ideas for Administrators

"To educate a man in mind and not in morale is to educate a menace to society."

—Theodore Roosevelt

In his book *Leading People*, Robert Rosen, PhD, describes the "healthy" organization:

> … a high performance enterprise that nurtures and taps the talents, ideas, and energy of its people. Healthy enterprises start from core human values, such as trust, integrity, and teamwork, and they balance the needs of all their stakeholders—employees, customers, shareholders, and the larger community. They don't do this because it's right or fair. They do it because it's better business, because it gives them the profound and enduring competitive advantage of a fast, flexible work culture where employees act like they own the business, learn on the job, and care deeply about quality and service (Rosen, 1997, pp. 5–6).

Suppose we reconstruct this paragraph for the *solution-focused school*:

> A solution-focused school nurtures and taps the talents, ideas, and energy of its students. The solution-focused school starts from core human values, such as trust, integrity, and teamwork, and the staff balances the needs of themselves, their students, their parents, and community. The staff does not do all of this because they want to raise test scores or earn notoriety. They do it because it gives them the profound and enduring opportunity of a fast, flexible school environment where students, staff, and parents act like they own the school, learn day to day, and care deeply about the quality of the students they graduate.

Chapter Nine was developed from researching managerial material and my personal involvement with constructing solution-focused schools through my consulting business. I have watched school counselors and school psychologists take solution-focused ideas into their counseling offices with great success. I've also heard firsthand of their struggles when they tried to share the ideas with their organization, a school, which did not share their vision. I have learned how much easier and effective creating such a school can be when *everyone* begins on the same page.

This chapter will provide the results of experience in implementing the ideas in this book into your organization, your school. I have provided hints and assistance for the administrator who desires something different for the next school year. There are reproducible handouts for your faculty meetings; steps to take to get every faculty member, parent, and student on the same track; and ideas for you to look inside of yourself to identify what your vision is for your school.

Creating the vision

Read the following excerpt and always remember it:

> People are not inspired by a higher net margin. They are not inspired by increased market share. And they are not inspired—at least not for very long—by a bigger paycheck. None of these things will cause them to achieve extraordinary goals or superior levels of performance. Something to believe in will (Rosen, 1996, p. 29).

When I began teaching in the early 1970s, I remember how each Fall all of the teachers from my district were summoned to a meeting that lasted several hours. We were returning back from a nice summer vacation and were immediately told what we were to accomplish during that school year. Back then, test scores were not an issue; student discipline was. Today, not only are test scores an issue; so are student discipline, social skills, parent involvement, drug abuse, adolescent drinking, career development, the list goes on and on. What is a teacher to do? Complain about having all of the expectations placed upon her without her expectations being heard? This is what makes many companies fail. This is why some of our schools are failing.

Instead, the solution-focused school year begins with a meeting where the administrator is convinced that a solution-focused approach will assist her students in achieving higher performance, better morale, and cooperation. However, she is cautious to stand up and say this because she knows that to achieve this, her teachers have to feel like the experts who can achieve it. So instead, she asks her teachers and staff members what they want. This becomes the vision for her school.

The solution-focused role play

Handout #1 will serve as a method to begin training. It is the most helpful exercise I use while training educators to learn the solution-focused theory in the classroom. Explain the following to the faculty members before passing out the handout:

"Please get into pairs. I would like one person to be a teacher and the other to be the most difficult student you worked with last year. Remember? For only two minutes, I want the student to be as difficult as possible and to talk about how he is disgusted with the way school is going this year. I'd like the teacher to find a way to convince the student that 'he has a problem'."

After two minutes, pass out the first handout and ask that only the teachers read the handout. The other person (the "student") should not see the handout. Tell the faculty that this will be a different approach but to still talk about the same problem as before. Instruct the faculty to start with the first question and use the questions to find solutions, differently.

Ask your faculty which scenario was more successful and why. Pass out the remaining handouts to those who portrayed the students. Ask the "students" what worked better for them in the second scenario. Ask the teachers what was different for them in the second scenario.

The meeting

After the role play, the administrator shares his ideas for a more successful school year and then asks the teachers and support staff for their ideas because he also believes that their ideas together will make the school work better.

Handout #1

Solution-Focused Questions

Ask the student the following questions:

1. "This sounds really awful. In fact, I'm surprised that things are not worse. How have you kept things from getting worse?"

2. "What will you be doing when things are better for you?"

3. "When was it that a little of that happened before, in the past?"

4. "What did you do to make that happen?"

5. "What do you do in other situations like that to help?"

6. "If I gave you a scale of 1–10, with '1' meaning the problem is really big and '10' meaning that you are bigger than the problem, where were you when we started talking?"

7. "Where are you now?"

8. "What could you do to move up just slightly on that scale this week?"

What does our school stand for?

What does this school believe in?

What does this school desire for each student?

How do our students perceive us?

How do the parents of our students perceive us?

Six months from now, what do you envision this school achieving?

Staff members may become stuck talking about what they do not want. That's okay. Simply redirect them by asking:

What do you want instead of that?

How do you think you could help to achieve that?

Who else do you think would help us to achieve that?

How have we, as a school, been able to succeed before?

Brainstorm Priorities: As teachers and staff members, what do you see as the four basic priorities that will help us to achieve what we have just discussed?

On an overhead projector, or a large chalkboard, draw the following chart as your teachers answer the brainstorming questions after the diagram. Make sure to number each "vision" and keep the "steps" specific and action oriented.

Vision	Actions	Current Strategy	Current Rating	6 weeks' Desired Rating	Steps
Example:					
students will be motivated to succeed	students will participate in classwork and want to learn	failure, consequences notes to parents, rewards	3	5	Talk to teachers who have success with challenging students, identify their strategies and use the strategy for a 3-week period.

Who on your team could begin to compile a list of teachers who could put together some strategies for your team to follow as an experiment?

This person will become part of a bigger team, The Solution Team, and will become a team member who will learn solution-focused ideas and take those ideas back to her team members and teach them how to approach students differently. The Solution Team will meet each week at a designated time and its members will receive comp time for attendance. The school counselor or school psychologist may be a likely addition to the team as instructors since the concepts of solution-focused teaching come from a counseling model. The administrator will then ask the faculty which teacher they would nominate to head the Solution Team, once trained. The administrator will meet with the instructors and leader and suggest readings such as this book, to understand the concepts of solution-focused teaching. The administrator will look in on those weekly training meetings and visit every team at least once every six weeks to learn how on track they are in becoming solution focused. He will continue visiting throughout the school year to let them know they have his total support and that he is interested in their ideas and their progress.

After the initial meeting the school secretary should compile the results of the first meeting onto handouts for the teachers and support staff. The handouts should be distributed to the teachers during the next few days, complete with the names of teachers who made suggestions, and the names of the Solution Team and Solution Team Instructors.

Additional handouts for the first faculty meeting

Distribute the next two handouts for the meeting in a folder to designate their importance and separateness from other paperwork. Mention that over the school year, the ideas in the folder will become clear.

Developing trust in your school

Trust in a new school program and approach such as this takes time to earn. Trust will be earned when the administrator follows through with the teacher's priorities and with his expectations of the Solution Team. The following are suggested attributes of administrators/leaders who desire to change a current program:

Handout #2
Guiding Ideas for Working with Students in the Solution-Focused School

1. Talk about students with a nonpathological approach. Describe their difficulties in a more positive way to make their problems solvable.

2. Do not worry about trying to figure out why a student is having a problem. Instead, watch for times when the problem is not there so much.

3. See students as people who are "stuck" in a problem, but are not the problem. This will make it easier to help them to escape from it.

4. When a student has a problem, ask the student what he or she wants to be different.

5. Remember, when you change your strategy, students change their behaviors.

6. Complex problems do not always call for complex solutions. Sometimes it just means we have a find problem-free times and learn what is different then.

7. When we step into our students' lives and try to understand where they are, we will have less resistance.

8. Motivation is necessary for change. Look for alternative, more positive ways to motivate students. Ask students what motivates them to learn.

9. If a lesson plan works, do it. If a lesson plan does not work, don't do it again. The same principle applies to behavioral interventions. Do something different!

10. Always focus on the possible and changeable when working with a student or parent. This will result in a solid goal that is achievable.

11. Go slowly to build successes. Think of making a slight change, not a big one.

12. Remember, rapid change can and does happen. Watch for changes and verbalize the changes to your students. Always ask them how they made even the smallest change.

13. Change is constant. It always happens when we do things differently.

14. Always watch for "exceptions" to problems. Notice what you are doing that helps the exceptions to happen. Notice what a student does or a parent does.

15. Change the time and the place so problems can't happen as they did before.

16. See problems differently, as an entity that influences a student, not as the student.

Handout #3

Suggestions for Talking to Students in the Solution-Focused School

Assisting Students with Conflict Resolution

The following suggested questions will assist you in helping your student(s) to find their own solutions and recognize their individual ability to solve problems. Your role is to simply help them to notice the times when there is no conflict.

1. "This sounds really awful. How have you managed to keep things together so far?"

2. "How would you like for things to be?"

Or, for dealing with more than one student:

"How would you both like things to be?"

3. "Think back to a time when things were better for you." (and school worked, home was better, friends were nicer, life was better, people weren't angry) "Tell me about those times. What was different then? What did you do that was different then?"

4. "What would you suggest doing today that worked before for you? What else? What else?"

5. "How could you think about this situation differently today so that doing something different was easier?"

Assisting Students Who Are Challenged Behaviorally

Students who act out are often defensive. The following questions will enable you to lower their defenses and resistance because they will allow you to step into their world and see what they see differently. This new comradeship with your students will help you to see your part in helping them to behave and put a new responsibility on the students to change your mind and the minds of others about their behavior.

1. "Who in your life sees you when you are doing things well?"

2. "When is it that school works for you and you feel slightly better about yourself?"

3. "Tell me about something that people don't always see in you."

4. "I see things in you that suggest to me that you can do whatever you want into school. It just seems you get off track easily. I wonder what small experiment you could for the rest of today that would begin to show others who you really are. I'm not sure what you will do. I will trust that you will do it anyway."

5. "I'm going to do something for you. I'm going to watch this afternoon for times when you behavior is under your control, not you under its control. I'll jot down what I see and you can take it home, okay?"

Handout #3 *(continued)*

Assisting Students Who Are Challenged Academically

There will always be students who have academic difficulties, but there is always hope, too. The following questions will enable you to help students identify better learning conditions and their learning style. Hopefully, you will discover with the students what other colleagues need to know to assist the students in succeeding.

1. Get the student's view of the problem and define a goal with her.

"This seems tough for you right now. How do you want things to be for yourself in school?"

"If I gave you a scale of 1–10, where '10' meant that things were going perfectly for you in school and a '1' meant that things were going very poorly, where would you place yourself at this time?"

"What would I see you doing just for this afternoon (elementary) or week (secondary) that would help you to move up just one small step on that scale? What specifically would that look like?"

If the student tell you what something else would be doing, agree with her and then say:

"I know, but we can't change him. What can you do so that things are better for **you**?"

2. Search for problem-free times with the student.

"Take me back to a time when this problem did not bother you and you passed (subject)."

"What did you do then that helped you to be more successful? How did you manage to do that?"

"Tell me what other teachers have done before that was really helpful to you?"

3. Compliment the student on any efforts that you have seen her take to work through the school problem.

"I've noticed that when I told everyone to turn in their spelling words yesterday, you were able to put them in the green box on my desk. Does it help for me to remind you? I will if you want me to."

4. Suggest a day when the problem was absent.

"Suppose you woke up tomorrow morning to discover that a miracle had taken place. Not only was school going well for you, but at home your parents were doing things that also helped you to be successful in school. What would they be doing differently?"

5. Designate a task.

"What do you think you should keep on doing that is working for you at this point?"

"From our talk today, what do you think would be a small step that you could take toward changing the way school is working for you?"

Be genuine

Be available. Step into classrooms and sit with the students. Let the teachers know you will be visiting their classrooms at random to watch their expertise in solution-focused teaching. Be sincere and write a thank-you note after you visit.

Be believable

When you promise your teachers to check on something for them, do so. It will increase your credibility. Let the teachers hear you talk to a student using solution-focused language.

Be dependable

Being there for your teachers does not mean you do everything for them with discipline or referrals. It does mean, however, that you offer your presence and your expertise in solution-focused teaching as support.

Be predictable

Staying consistent with any program is vital since it reinforces your commitment to the program. When you are committed, your faculty will eventually be committed. If you allow certain teachers to send students to your office for you to fix, the other teachers will expect the same. Trust them. They will become more competent when you pretend to be less competent.

Be benevolent

The outcome of the whole picture is your goal. The horizon predicts a beautiful sunset where teachers see their students differently and the students see themselves differently. This will happen when your goal is for the whole community, not just to curtail discipline or increase academic performance.

Gaining participation

If vision provides the direction, and trust creates the safe foundation, then participation is the fuel that drives the organization forward. This power is found lying dormant in the hearts and imaginations of the people inside the company. (Rosen, p. 111)

I once worked for a psychiatric hospital and encountered one of the best nurse managers I have ever met. One of her employees told me that once during a long holiday, there was a problem on the unit. She called her manager at home to find out what to do. Instead of telling the nurse what to do, the nurse manager said:

"What do you think would solve the problem right now?"

"What would be the first thing you could do to make that happen?"

"Whose assistance there on the floor could help you out?"

The nurse conveying the story to me smiled and relayed how confident the nurse manager had made her and how proud she felt to have been given some control during the crisis.

This same principle works for teachers and support staff as well. Give them power, and believe that they can solve the problems they bring to you. Support them by asking them to bring the student to you and request that the teacher stay and work out the differences with the student in your office *together*. If this does not happen, the student will be punished or talked to and will return to the same system with which he got in trouble. This results in relapse, relapse, relapse. However, when the relationship changes, the system—as well as perceptions and reactions—will change. Eventually, teachers will learn what the nurse learned—that they can solve their own problems. Until then, create the context for them to begin training.

Teacher evaluations

Utilize your competency evaluation of teachers to encourage your faculty to study the solution-focused ideas in this book. Select someone from your Solution Team, such as the school counselor or school psychologist, who grasps the solution-focused concepts and utilize their expertise as instructors of those who need brushing up on the ideas. While voluntary participation is always welcomed, teachers sometimes need extra incentives to increase their participation. Knowing that their evaluations will include identifying solution-focused teaching and relationship strategies, can motivate teachers to learn them. If expecting competency works, do more of it.

Learn, always learn

Learning is an investment. Make learning solution-focused ideas fun for your teachers and support staff. Show a portion of the following two films during your first meeting and ask the teachers what happens in the video excerpts.

Pre-meeting video: City Slickers

Show the portion where Billy Crystal and his two friends are herding cattle after Curly's funeral. As the three talk about "good days" and "bad days", see how their redescription sheds a new light on all of their problems. When teachers think differently about their students and less about the "bad days", their students will respond differently.

Post-meeting video: Mr. Holland's Opus

Show the portion where Mr. Holland encounters Ms. Lane, a red-haired clarinet player who is thinking of giving up the clarinet because she feels incompetent. As Mr. Holland plays a record of "Louie Louie", he describes how music should be fun and have heart. When teachers find a way into their students' resources as Mr. Holland did, the students blossom and the sky is the limit.

Listen to your faculty as they begin their journey into the program. Listen for what they learn. Walk by their classrooms and listen for good lesson plans, kind conversations, and teachers trying to reach the troubled gang member in the lunchroom. Recognize their efforts and write them notes like the one here:

Dear Ms Santosian,

This afternoon I walked along the hallway to find you and Andre talking seriously about his involvement with a gang. I watched as you seemed to sincere in coaxing him into studying a chapter on World War II. He seemed to appreciate the time you took to talk to him outside of class. I appreciate your efforts as well. I am proud to be in a school with someone as invested as you are.

Sincerely,

Mrs. Thomas, Vice Principal

Copy one of the dialogues found throughout this book that seems to fit your school population. Choose faculty members to read the dialogue and discuss why the dialogue led to solutions.

Cultivating creativity

Successful leaders focus first on their own natural strengths and discover their creative potential, making it easier for them to unleash the creativity of others. Such leaders hire people who are flexible and inquisitive. They help employees discover their own talents, and they link those talents to the task at hand. Then the best leaders create the right environment for people to experiment, take risks, and fulfill their creative potential. (Rosen, p. 246)

Creativity doesn't just happen. Someone asks "What if?" and someone else says, "Okay, maybe we could do it this way." This is how the Walt Disney Company has become so successful. First, its leaders identify the unique talent in each employee. Second, the leader then structures the job to nurture the creativity. Certain rules are eliminated and flexibility replaces procedures that have not been productive. Third, the leader structures an environment that supports risk taking and experimenting.

Schools were always meant to be flexible and creative. They were always meant to be the forerunners of teaching productivity, not stagnation. Assisting teachers and support staff members to use their individual skills and resources to make the solution-focused school *work* is no different. Go to your staff and present them with a problem and ask for their assistance since they are out "in the trenches". Let them know you will anxiously await their answer. Then, put their answers into place and call attention to their accomplishment.

Promoting integrity

There may be a few teachers in your school who will resist the solution-focused school. They may feel that students need to be sent to administrators and not dealt with in the classroom. They may feel that students who need special education cannot be helped in their classroom. Hear them as inexperienced in the new program. Change is scary to people. Teachers typically like structure and resist change because it disrupts the way things work. Because of this, tread softly when you meet resistance. Listen to these teachers' complaints and acknowledge that change is difficult. Then, redirect these teachers to the fact that the majority of the faculty are working hard to promote such a new program. Ask them to watch over the next week for anything they find acceptable about the program. Meet with them again and listen to their discoveries.

Notice how this theme keeps circulating with students, parents, and teachers. The solution-focused model is more than questions. It is more than strategies and wording things differently. It is about viewing the world and those in it as people struggling to feel competent. When teachers feel competent in one system and the system changes, they feel incompetent. Help those who complain to be competent and you will win them over, I promise. They simply need to understand the program.

Concluding comments

Humans gather together in places where they feel they belong. They look for acceptance, validity, similarities, and safety. The solution-focused school thrives on acceptance of its students and parents as persons in need of direction. The school validates those who feel invalid. The staff provides safety and a belief in making tomorrow a better day for our youth. What keeps such a community together? Leaders such as you. They need you to keep them on track. When your school begins promoting the very different ideas of solution-focused teaching, you will find that parents and community leaders are refreshed to find a new approach in the making. The community will be relieved that someone has taken the risk to stand up and say, "I think we need a positive approach and I am interested in how you think we can do that."

Our communities are laden with people who desire relationships and learning new ways of living. Perhaps the solution-focused school should include such ideas in its community offerings. The school was once looked to as a pillar in the community. Why not offer what parents find important. One way is to ask them through surveys or interviews. Solution-focused teaching is, after all, a model for focusing on what works in life.

The author presents workshops to schools and communities who desire assistance in becoming solution focused. She also welcomes your letters of success! Write to her and describe how solution-focused teaching has made a difference in your school.

Linda Metcalf, PhD
5126 Bridgewater Drive
Arlington, Texas 76017

Appendix

Notes to keep on teacher's desks:

Teacher's 3 x 5 Ready Reference to Solutions

1. This sounds awful. How will you know when things are better?

2. When were you able to do that last?

3. How did you do that?

4. How could you do just a little of that today?

5. On a scale of 1–10, where are you?

Ready Reference of Solution-Focused Ideas

1. Changing the description of the problem will help me design new strategies. There is always an exception.

2. Students get stuck in problems ... they are not problems themselves.

3. There is a snowball effect when I change.

4. Work on the student's goal, no matter how different it is from mine.

When you meet resistance, find a way to cooperate.

Notice when school works today.

This is a Solution-Focused School.

We stand behind our students' abilities.

An exceptional solution-focused teacher teaches in this classroom.

school logo

You

are

about

to be

discovered!

Come in!

Bibliography

Ageland, J. and Glanze, W., 1987, *Pearls of Wisdom*, Harper & Row, New York.

American Psychiatric Association, 1997, *Desk Reference to the Diagnostic Criteria from DSM-IV*, Washington, D.C.

Bluestein, J., 1995, *Mentors, Masters and Mrs. MacGregor*, Health Communications Inc., Deerfield Beach.

Cade, B. and O'Hanlon, W., *1993, A Brief Guide to Brief Therapy*, W.W. Norton, New York.

Campbell, C. and Dahir, C, 1997, *The National Standards for School Counseling Programs*, American School Counselor Association, Alexandria, VA.

Chapman, J. and Boersma, F., 1979, Learning disabilities, locus of control, and mother attitudes, *Journal of Educational Psychology*, 71, pp. 250–258.

Combs, G. and Freedman, J., 1990, *Symbol, Story and Ceremony*, W. W. Norton & Company, New York/London.

De Shazer, S., 1985, *Keys to Solutions in Brief Therapy*, W.W. Norton , New York.

De Shazer, S., 1985, *Clues: Investigating Solutions in Brief Therapy*, W. W. Norton, New York and London.

De Shazer, S., 1988, *Putting Difference to Work*, W.W. Norton, New York and London.

Durrant, M., 1993, *Residential Treatment*, W.W. Norton, New York.

Durrant, M., 1995, *Creative Strategies for School Problems*, W.W. Norton, New York.

Epston, D., 1989, *Collected Papers*, Dulwich Centre Publications, Adelaide, South Australia.

Epston, D. and White, M., 1990, *Narrative Means to Therapeutic Ends*, W.W. Norton, New York.

Finkelhor, D. and Dziuba-Leatherman, J., 1988, Victimization of children, *American Psychologist*, 49, pp. 173–183 (1994).

Freeman, C., 1988, *The Teachers' Book of Wisdom*, Walnut Grove Press, Nashville.

Furman, B. and Tapani, A., 1997, *Reteaming—Succeeding Together*, Snellman Printing House, Helsinki.

Harwell, J., 1995, *Ready-to-Use Information and Materials for Assessing Specific Learning Disabilitie*s, The Center for Applied Research in Education, West Nyack, NY.

Johnson, L., 1993, *Dangerous Minds*, St. Martin's Paperbacks, New York.

Keeney, B, 1994, Conference remarks, Fort Worth, Texas.

Lee, H., 1988, *To Kill a Mockingbird*, re-issue edition, Little Brown & Company.

Lipchik, E. and De Shazer, S., Purposeful sequences for beginning the solution-focused interview, in E. Lipchik, 1988, *Interviewing*, Aspen, Rockville, MD, pp. 105–117.

Metcalf, L., 1991, Therapy with parent–adolescent conflict: Creating a climate in which clients can figure what to do differently, *Family Therapy Case Studies*, 6 (2), pp. 25–34.

Metcalf, L., 1995, *Counseling Toward Solutions*, The Center for Applied Research in Education, West Nyack, NY.

Metcalf, L., 1997, *Parenting Toward Solutions*, The Center for Applied Research in Education, West Nyack, NY.

Metcalf, L. and Thomas, F., Client and therapist perceptions of solution focused brief therapy: A qualitative analysis, 1994, *Journal of Family Psychotherapy*, 5 (4), pp. 49–66.

O'Hanlon, W.H. and Weiner-Davis, M., 1989, *In Search of Solutions*, W.W. Norton, New York.

O'Hanlon, W.H. and Weiner-Davis, M., 1996, Informational sheets from *Possibilities*, Santa Fe, New Mexico.

Rosen, R., 1996, *Leading People*, Penguin Books, New York.

Ruenzel, D., 1994, Playing by the rules, *Teacher Magazine*, November/December, pp. 32–37.

Scannell, E., 1980, *Games Trainers Play*, McGraw Hill, New York.

Shaffer, D., 1996, *Developmental Psychology*, Brooks/Cole Publishing Company, Pacific Grove, CA.

Sternberg, R., 1997, Still smarting, *Teacher Magazine*, January, pp. 40–41.

Trickett, P. and Putnam, F., 1993, Impact of child sexual abuse on females: Toward a developmental, psychobiological integration, *Psychological Science*, 4, pp. 81–87.

Weisman, J., 1994, Full speed ahead, *Teacher Magazine*, November/December, pp. 44–49.

White, M., 1989, Saying hullo again: The incorporation of the lost relationship in the resolution of grief, *Selected Papers*, Dulwich Centre Publications, Adelaide, South Australia.

Wolfner, G. and Gelles, R., 1993, A profile of violence toward children: A national study, *Child Abuse and Neglect*, 17, pp. 197–212.

Wulf, S., 1997, How to teach our children well, *Time Magazine*, October, pp. 62–69.